A MANUAL
OF
SANSKRIT PHONETICS

A MANUAL
OF
SANSKRIT PHONETICS

In Comparison with the Indogermanic Mother-Language, for Students of Germanic and Classical Philology,

by

Dr. C. C. UHLENBECK,

ENGLISH EDITION BY THE AUTHOR

GYAN

Published by

Gyan Publishing House
5, Ansari Road
Daryaganj, New Delhi-110002
Phone: 011-47034999, 9811692060
E-mail: books@gyanbooks.com

Distribution Network
gyanbooks.com
India, USA, Canada, UK, Australia, France

ISBN : 978-81-212-9954-1 (PB)
First Published, 1898

2nd Impression 2021

Printed at: Gyan Press, Delhi.

A Manual of Sanskrit Phonetics
Author: Dr. C. C. Uhlenbeck,

A MANUAL

OF

SANSKRIT PHONETICS.

IN COMPARISON WITH THE INDOGERMANIC MOTHER-LANGUAGE, FOR STUDENTS OF GERMANIC AND CLASSICAL PHILOLOGY,

BY

Dr. C. C. UHLENBECK,

Extraord. Professor of Sanskrit and Comparative Philology in the University of Amsterdam.

ENGLISH EDITION BY THE AUTHOR.

LONDON:
LUZAC & Co.
Publishers to the India Office.
46, Great Russell Street.
1898.

PREFACE.

The idea of publishing an English edition of my *Handboek der Indische Klankleer* (Leiden, Blankenberg & C°. 1894) was suggested to me by others; but for that suggestion this translation certainly would not have been undertaken. In general I have followed the Dutch text: alterations have been made only, when there were positive inaccuracies in the Dutch edition or when an alteration had become necessary because of the progress of comparative philology since 1894. I have also considerably augmented the references to the scientific literature and somewhat enlarged the part on the accent. Some emendations are due to the recensions of Kern, Speyer, Zubatý [and Johansson], of whose observations and remarks I have made a grateful use.

I further need only repeat, what I said in the preface to the Dutch original: the purpose of my having composed this little handbook is to introduce the student into the comparative-phonetic study of Sanskrit. Though as a rule students of Classical and Germanic philology do not read Vedic texts, I have not hesitated to cite words and forms, which had already become obsolete in the epic and classical language, mentioning, of course, the fact, that such a word only occurs in Vedic. In general I have avoided to cite Iranic, Lithuanian and Slavonic: I know, it is true, that this lessens the scientific worth of my book, but I do not think it desirable to trouble the student with several languages, which are either quite unknown to him or which he only just begins to learn.

May this edition be of some use to the students in England, America and India.

Amsterdam, Nov. 1897. C. C. UHLENBECK.

CONTENTS.

Liquids.

Labial explosives.

Dental explosives.

Guttural explosives.

Palatal explosives.

Spirants.

B. The relation of the Indian consonants to the Indogermanic.

Semivowels.

Nasals.

Liquids.

Labial explosives.

Dental explosives.

Lingual explosives.

Guttural explosives.

Palatal affricates.

Spirants.

PART III. SANDHI-SYSTEM.

PART IV. ACCENT.

INTRODUCTION.

§ 1. **The Indogermanic family of languages.** The great family of languages, to which Sanskrit belongs, is called the Indogermanic, Indoceltic or Aryan. I prefer the first name, because it is the most usual, though the name *Indoceltic* may claim a greater accuracy. The word *Indogermanic* dates from a time, when it was not yet proved, that the Celtic dialects also make part of our family of languages, and indicates by the combined name of the utmost branches, Indian and Germanic, the whole territory of speech, to which they belong. Now that it is certain, that Celtic also is a member of our family, it would be accurate to replace the word *Indogermanic* by *Indoceltic*, because not Germanic, but Celtic is the utmost branch to the Occident. The name *Indogermanic* however is generally adopted and it would be impossible to supplant it by another. By the word *Aryan* is generally understood a certain subdivision of the Indogermanic family, viz. the Indo-Iranian, and therefore it would seem unsuitable to use this name also for the whole Indogermanic family. See G. Meyer, Idg. forschungen 2, 125 sqq. and Spiegel, Die Arische periode (Leipzig 1887) VI sq.

The Indogermanic family consists of the following nine groups:

1. *Aryan*, see § 2.

2. *Armenian.*

3. *Phrygian-Thracian*, only known from proper names, glosses and inscriptions.

4. *Albanian.*

5. *Greek.*

6. *Italic*, which comprises not only ancient languages of Italy (Latin, Oscian, Umbrian, Samnitic), but also the modern dialects, which have sprung from popular Latin.

7. *Celtic*, which is divided into Gallic (the extinct language of ancient Gallia), Britannian (Cymric or Welsh, Cornish, Bas-Breton) and Gaelic (Scotch, Irish, Manx).

8. *Germanic*, which is commonly divided into an eastern and a western group. The eastern comprehends Gothic and Scandinavian (Icelandic, Danish, Norwegian, Swedish); to the western belong English (in its oldest literary period called Anglosaxon), Frisian and German (High-German and Low-German)

9. *Balto-Slavonic*, which consists of two groups, the Baltic and the Slavonic. The former is divided into Old-Prussian, Lithuanian and Lettish; the latter comprehends Southern-Slavonic (Ecclesiastical-Slavonic, Slovenian, Servo-Croatian, Bulgarian), Russian (Great-Russian, White-Russian, Little-Russian) and Western-Slavonic (Polish, Wendish, Bohemian and the extinct Polabic).

About the mutual relations of these groups see J. Schmidt, Die verwandtschaftsverhältnisse der Indogermanischen sprachen (Weimar 1872) and cf. Brugmann, Zur frage nach den verwandtschaftsverhältnissen der Indogermanischen sprachen (Techmer's Internationale Zeitschr. für allgemeine sprachwissenschaft 1, 226 sqq.).

§ 2. **The Aryan group.** The Aryan group is divided into two subdivisions:

1. *Indian*, see § 3.

2. *Iranian.*

Ancient Iranian is handed down to us in two dialects, viz. Avestian and Old-Persian. Avestian is the language of the Avesta, the sacred book of the Parsis. The oldest parts of this Zoroastrian bible date back to many centuries before Christ, and their language is more archaic than the classical dialect of the younger Avesta. This oldest Avestian is called the *Gāthā*-dialect. In Old-Persian we have only the cuneiform inscriptions of the Achaemenidian kings, the oldest of which is that of Darius Hystaspes at Behistān and dates from ± 520 before Christ. Numerous inscriptions are found on and near the ruins of Persepolis: the youngest of them is of the middle of the fourth century before Christ. See Bartholomae, Handbuch der Altiranischen dialekte (Leipzig 1883), Vorgeschichte der Iranischen sprachen (Grundriss der Iranischen philologie I); Williams Jackson, An Avesta grammar (Part I, Stuttgart 1892); Spiegel, Die Altpersischen Keilinschriften [2] (Leipzig 1881).

The language of the Sassanidian period is called Middle-Persian, Pahlavī or Huzvāresh. The modern Iranian dialects are New-Persian, Kurdish, Ossetic, Afghan, Balūčī &c. Some of the principal works on these languages are: Horn, Grundriss der Neupersischen etymologie (Strassburg 1893); Hübschmann, Persische studien (Strassburg 1895), Etymologie und lautlehre der Ossetischen sprache (Strassburg 1887); Justi, Kurdische grammatik (Petersburg 1880); Trumpp, Grammar of the Paštō (= Afghan, London 1873); Geiger, Etymologie des Balūčī (München 1890), Lautlehre des Balūčī (München 1891); Tomaschek, die Pamir-dialekte (Wien 1880).

§ 3. **The Indian dialects.** In the first place is to be

mentioned the Vedic dialect, which was spoken in the Panjāb and in Kābulistān ± 1500 before Christ. Here arose the greater part of the *ṛc*-hymns, which in a later period, when the Indo-Aryans had spread more to the East, were collected into the Ṛgvedasaṁhitā. From this time dates the greater part of the Vedic literature.

From an Indian dialect of the Veda-period sprang the *saṁskṛtā bhāṣā* (adorned, elaborated language) of Madhyadeça (the Midland, on the upper course of the Gaṅgā and Yamunā), which some centuries before Christ must have been a living language, be it not in quite the same form as in most of the literary Sanskrit works. To the time, when Sanskrit was yet living as a popular language, we may refer at least the bulk of the great epic poems Mahābhārata and Rāmāyaṇa. There are several reasons to assume that this spoken Sanskrit descends from an other Old-Indian dialect than that of the Vedic hymns (cf. § 43). The most indispensable books for Sanskrit students are: Whitney, A Sanskrit grammar [3] (Leipzig 1896), The roots, verb-forms and primary derivatives of the Sanskrit language (Leipzig 1885); Wackernagel, Altindische grammatik I (Göttingen 1896); Böhtlingk & Roth, Sanskritwörterbuch (Petersburg 1855—1875). See also the list of books in Lanman's Sanskrit reader (Boston 1888), XVII sqq.

While Sanskrit continued as the language of the learned and educated, there arose numerous popular dialects or Prākrit's (*prākṛtā bhāṣā*, ordinary language), many of which are known to us, partly from separate works, partly from Sanskrit plays (fifth, sixth and following centuries after Christ). At how early a time Sanskrit can no longer have been a popular language, appears from the Prākrit inscriptions of Açoka, king of Pāṭaliputra, who reigned from 259 till 222 before

Christ. Particularly interesting is that Prākrit, in which the sacred books of the southern Buddhists are written and which is called *Pāli*. Kern (Geschiedenis van het Buddhisme in Indië, Haarlem 1882—1884, 2, 339) says, that Pāli is a dialect, the place of which is not yet fixed with entire certainty, but that at all events it was not the language of Açoka and the kingdom of Magadha. Oldenberg (Buddha, Berlin 1881, 76) thinks, that Pāli was once the popular language of southern India. See about the ancient popular dialects of India Lassen, Institutiones linguae Pracriticae (Bonnae 1837); Jacobi, Ausgewählte erzählungen in Mahārāṣṭrī (Leipzig 1886); Ernst Kuhn, Beiträge zur Pāli-grammatik (Berlin 1875) and other works.

From these Prākrits descend the modern Aryan vernaculars of India: Hindī (intermixed with numberless Persian and Arabian words it is called Hindustānī or Urdū), Panjābī, Sindhī, Gujarāṭī, Marāṭhī, Oriya, Bengālī &c. See Beames, A comparative grammar of the modern Aryan languages of India (London 1872—1879).

§ 4. **Sounds and letters.** The oldest Indian writing, that is known to us, is found in the inscriptions of Açoka: here we distinguish two different systems of characters, one of which has been evidently derived from a Semitic alphabet and the other may be of the same origin. From the latter descend the younger Indian alphabets, to which belongs Devanāgarī, properly the alphabet of Hindustān. The natives of India write Sanskrit in different modes, but by western scholars Devanāgarī is only used.

Here I give a list of the Sanskrit letters, according to the most usual system of transliteration: each character has always the same phonetic value and all sounds of the language are represented by a separate character.

Vowels.

a, ā, i, ī, u, ū.
e, o.
ṛ, ṝ, ḷ, ḹ.

Diphthongs.

āi, āu.

Mutes.

Gutturals: *k, kh, g, gh.*
Linguals: *ṭ, ṭh, ḍ, ḍh.*
Dentals: *t, th, d, dh.*
Labials: *p, ph, b, bh.*

Palatal affricates.

c, ch, j, jh.

Nasals.

ṅ, ñ, ṇ, n, m and the anusvāra and anunāsika, which in transliteration are both written *ṁ*.

Liquids.

r, l.

Semivowels.

y, v.

Sibilants.

ç, ṣ, s.

Aspiration.

h and the visarga *ḥ*.

The usual order of arrangement is slightly different from that given above.

A few words must be said on the phonetic value of the Devanāgarī letters.

The *a*, *i* and *u* are short vowels: their pronunciation is nearly the same as in German. The corresponding long vowels are *ā*, *ī*, *ū*.

The *e* and *o* are long vowels with a narrow pronunciation: they are contractions of *ai* and *au*.

The *ṛ* and *ḷ* are sonant liquids; *ṝ* and *ḹ* are the corresponding long ones, but *ḹ* does not occur in a single genuine Sanskrit word.

The *āi* and *āu* are diphthongs: their first component *ā* is long, the second components are the semivowels *i̯* and *u̯*.

The *k* and *g* are the ordinary European *k*- and *g*-sounds. Their corresponding aspirates are *kh* (*k* + *h*) and *gh* (*g* + *h*).

The *ṭ* and *ḍ* are distinguished from the dentals by turning up the tip of the tongue to the palate. Their corresponding aspirates are *ṭh* (*ṭ* + *h*) and *ḍh* (*ḍ* + *h*).

The *t* and *d* are ordinary dentals, i. e. they are formed by turning up the tip of the tongue to the upper teeth. Their corresponding aspirates are *th* (*t* + *h*) and *dh* (*d* + *h*).

The *p* and *b* are ordinary labials and *ph* (*p* + *h*) and *bh* (*b* + *h*) are their corresponding aspirates.

The *c* and *j* are palatal affricates: *c* consists of *t* + *ś* and *j* of *d* + *ź*. Engl. *ch* in *chaff*, *chain*, *choose*, *churl* and *g*, *j* in *gem*, *gentleman*, *gin*, *jail*, *jam*, *jest*, *jockey* are nearly the same sounds.

Each of the nasals is akin to one of the series of consonants given above: the *ṅ* is guttural (= engl. *ng* in *long*, *sing*), the *ṇ* lingual, the *n* dental, the *m* labial and the *ñ* palatal. By *ṁ* (anusvāra and anunāsika) is indicated the nasal pronunciation of a preceding vowel.

The *r* must have been a lingual sound, because it has the power to lingualize neighbouring dentals. The *l* is a dental sound.

The *y* is a semivowel, which is closely related to the vowel *i*; i. e. it is a consonant *i* like engl. *y* in *year*, *yard*, *yoke*. The *v* originally stood in the same relation to *u* and had the sound of engl. *w* in *wall*, *word*, *wear*; but from an early time it was changed to a spirant (engl. *v* in *veil*, *vain*, *vine*), except when preceded by a consonant in the same syllable.

The *ç* is palatal like engl. *sh* in *short*, *shield*, *shut*. The *ṣ* is lingual and distinguished from the *s* in the same way as *ṭ*, *ḍ*, *ṇ* from *t*, *d*, *n*. The *s* is our ordinary surd *s*.

By *h* and *ḥ* are understood our usual *h* (spiritus asper), but the visarga (*ḥ*) is usually neglected by us in the pronunciation of Sanskrit words.

PART I.

SYSTEM OF VOWELS.

A. The representation of the Indogermanic vowels in Sanskrit.

§ 5. **The Indogermanic vowels in general.** There was a great variety of vowels in the mother-language, but their accurate pronunciation is not definable. We indicate these vowels by the following letters:

a, *ā*; *e*, *ē*; *o*, *ō*; *ə*; *i*, *ī*; *u*, *ū*.

The *e*, *ē*, *o*, *ō* had a broad pronunciation. The *ə* was perhaps something between *a* and engl. *e* in *oldest*, *father*.

There were also sonant nasals and liquids, which are written *m̥*, *n̥*, *r̥*; *l̥*. We understand by *n̥* not only the dental *n*-sonans, but also the palatal and guttural sonant nasals. Some scholars deny the existence of these sounds in the mother-language: see Bechtel, Die hauptprobleme der Indogermanischen lautlehre seit Schleicher (Göttingen 1892), 114 sqq. and J. Schmidt, Kritik der sonantentheorie (Weimar 1895), cf. Hirt, Idg. forschungen 7, 147 sqq.

Combinations of vowels with semivowels, nasals and liquids were very common:

ai̯, *āi̯*, *ei̯*, *ēi̯*, *oi̯*, *ōi̯*;
au̯, *āu̯*, *eu̯*, *ēu̯*, *ou̯*, *ōu̯*;
am, *ām*, *em*, *ēm*, *om*, *ōm*, *əm*;
an, *ān*, *en*, *ēn*, *on*, *ōn*, *ən*;
ar, *ār*, *er*, *ēr*, *or*, *ōr*, *ər*;
al, *āl*, *el*, *ēl*, *ol*, *ōl*, *əl*.

Many scholars assume, that there were also long sonant nasals and liquids in the mother-language. See de Saussure, Mémoire sur le système primitif des voyelles dans les langues Indo-Européennes (Paris 1887), 262 sqq. and Brugmann, Grundriss der vergleichenden grammatik der Indogermanischen sprachen (Strassburg 1886—1893), 1, 208 sq. 243 sqq.: against this theory Bechtel 203 sqq.

§ 6. **The Indogermanic vowel-gradation.** The Indogermanic mother-language had four series of vowels, based on *e*, *ē*, *ā* and *ō*. De Saussure 134 sqq. has tried to prove, that the long base-vowels *ē*, *ā*, *ō* are contractions of *e* with a short vowel and considers the *ē*-, *ā*- and *ō*-series only as special cases of the *e*-series.

Hübschmann, Das Indogermanische vocalsystem (Strassburg 1885), Brugmann 1, 248 sqq., Bartholomae, Bezz. Beitr. 17, 91 sqq. and others assume an *a*-series and an *o*-series besides the four given above. Against this opinion Bechtel 256 sqq.

The base-vowels *e*, *ē*, *ā*, *ō* were weakened in all syllables, which had but a slight accent or no accent at all. In the latter case the radical vowel was lost without leaving any trace, but in syllables with a slight accent *e* was reduced to *ə* (Bartholomae, Bezz. Beitr. 17, 109 sqq., cf. also skr. *timirá-s* ‘dark’: *támas* ‘darkness’), *ē* to *e* or *ə*, *ā* to *a* or *ə*, *ō* to *o* or *ə* (Bechtel 248).

But a regular vowel-exchange is found also in accentuated

syllables: so we have an *ablaut* *e* : *o*, *ē* : *ō*, *ā* : *ō*, but the base-vowel *ō* is not met with in a modified form. The causes of this *ablaut* are not yet clear. Kretschmer (Kuhn's Zeitschr. 31, 366 sqq.) has shown, that G. Meyer's way of explaining it (Kuhn's Zeitschr. 24, 227 sqq.) can not be the right one.

The base-vowel *e* (*o*) often was lengthened to *ē* (*ō*): Streitberg (Idg. forschungen 3, 305 sqq.) has tried to explain this phenomenon. I see no reason to admit with Bartholomae, that there was also a *dehnstufe* of *ē*, *ā*, *ō*.

I. *e*-series.

	Weak:	Strong:	Lengthened:
A.	— , *ə*.	*e*, *o*.	*ē*, *ō*.
B.	*i̯* (*i*), *ī*.	*ei̯* (*i̯e*), *oi̯* (*i̯o*).	*ēi̯* (*i̯ē*), *ōi̯* (*i̯ō*).
C.	*u̯* (*u*), *ū*.	*eu̯* (*u̯e*), *ou̯* (*u̯o*).	*ēu̯* (*u̯ē*), *ōu̯* (*u̯ō*).
D.	*m* (*m̥*), *əm* (*mə*).	*em* (*me*), *om* (*mo*).	*ēm* (*mē*), *ōm* (*mō*).
E.	*n* (*n̥*), *ən* (*nə*).	*en* (*ne*), *on* (*no*).	*ēn* (*nē*), *ōn* (*nō*).
F.	*r* (*r̥*), *ər* (*rə*).	*er* (*re*), *or* (*ro*).	*ēr* (*rē*), *ōr* (*rō*).
G.	*l* (*l̥*), *əl* (*lə*).	*el* (*le*), *ol* (*lo*).	*ēl* (*lē*), *ōl* (*lō*).

When *e* was lost before (or after) *i̯*, *u̯*, *m*, *n*, *r*, *l* these semivowels, nasals and liquids remained consonant before vowels, but became sonant before consonants. Concerning *ī*, *ū*, *əm*, *ən*, *ər*, *əl* must be observed, that they occur not only as *ə*-degree of *ei̯*, *eu̯*, *em*, *en*, *er*, *el*, but also as weakest degree of *ei̯e*, *eu̯e*, *eme*, *ene*, *ere*, *ele*: see de Saussure 239 sqq.; Brugmann 1, 104 sqq.; Bartholomae, Bezz. Beitr. 17, 109 sqq. I assume with Bartholomae, that *ī* and *ū* are contractions of *ə* + *i̯* and *ə* + *u̯* and stand on a level with *əm*, *ən*, *ər*, *əl*.

II. *ē*-series.

	Weak:	Strong:
A.	— , *ə*, *e*.	*ē*, *ō*.
B.	*i̯* (*i*), *ī*, *ei̯* (*i̯e*).	*ēi̯* (*i̯ē*), *ōi̯* (*i̯ō*).
C.	*u̯* (*u*), *ū*, *eu̯* (*u̯e*).	*ēu̯* (*u̯ē*), *ōu̯* (*u̯ō*).

The relation of *i̯*, *u̯* to *i*, *u* in *ēi̯*- (*i̯ē*-) and *ēu̯*- (*u̯ē*-) roots is the same as in *ei̯*- (*i̯e*-) and *eu̯*- (*u̯e*-) roots: we find *i̯*, *u̯* before vowels and *i*, *u* before consonants. About the *ēi̯*- and *ēu̯*-roots see Schulze, Kuhn's Zeitschr. 27, 420 sqq.; Wiedemann, Das Litauische praeteritum (Strassburg 1891), 25 sqq. 32.

III. *ā*-series.

	Weak:	Strong:
A.	— , *ə*, *a*.	*ā*, *ō*.
B.	*i̯* (*i*), *ī*, *ai̯* (*i̯a*).	*āi̯* (*i̯ā*), *ōi̯* (*i̯ō*).
C.	*u̯* (*u*), *ū*, *au̯* (*u̯a*).	*āu̯* (*u̯ā*), *ōu̯* (*u̯ō*).

Concerning the roots with *i̯*, *u̯* we must observe, that the mutual relation of *i̯*, *u̯* and *i*, *u* in the weakest degree is the same as in the *e*- and *ē*-series. About the *ablaut* in *āi̯*- and *āu̯*-roots see Schulze, Kuhn's Zeitschr. 27, 420 sqq.; Kretschmer, Kuhn's Zeitschr. 31, 385 sqq.; Wiedemann 29. 32 sq.

IV. *ō*-series.

	Weak:	Strong:
A.	— , *ə*, *o*.	*ō*.
B.	*i̯* (*i*), *ī*, *oi̯*.	*ōi̯*.
C.	*u̯* (*u*), *ū*, *ou̯*.	*ōu̯*.

The relation of *i̯*, *u̯* to *i*, *u* in the weakest degree of roots with *i̯*, *u̯* is the same as in the *e*-, *ē*- and *ā*-series. About the *ōi̯*- and *ōu̯*-roots see Schulze, Kuhn's Zeitschr. 27, 420 sqq.;

Kretschmer, Kuhn's Zeitschr. 31, 385 sqq.; Wiedemann 29, 33 sqq.; Bechtel 274.

Examples of the vowel-gradation.

I. *e*-series.

The noun-stem **ped-*. Weak: ved. *upabdá-*, trampling, noise, avest. *frabda-*, fore part of the foot, gr. ἐπίβδαι, the day after a festival. Against our expectation we find the unweakened *e* in the gen. sing. skr. *padás*, lat. *pedis*. Strong: gr. πόδα. Lengthened: lat. *pēs*; gr. dor. πώς, goth. *fōtus*, skr. acc. sing. *pā́dam*, nom. sing. *pā́t*.

The suffix *-ter-*, for instance in **pəter-*. Weak: gen. sing. gr. πατρός, goth. *fadrs*; loc. plur. skr. *pitṛ́ṣu*, gr. πατράσι. Strong: acc. sing. skr. *pitáram*, gr. πατέρα; gr. εὐπάτορα. Lengthened: nom. sing. skr. *pitā́*, gr. πατήρ; gr. εὐπάτωρ.

Also the suffixes *-en-*, *-men-* (weak before vowels *-n-*, *-mn-*; before consonants *-n̥-*, *-mn̥-*) and numerous verbal roots as **pet-*, to fly, **bhei̯d-*, to split, **bheu̯dh-*, to perceive, **gem-*, to go, **men-*, to think, **bher-*, to bear, **kel-*, to raise up.

II. *ē*-series.

The root **dhē-*, to put. Weak: 1 pers. plur. praes. ind. act. skr. *dadhmás*; part. perf. pass. skr. *-dhita-s*, *hitá-s*, lat. *crēditus*; gr. θετός, ἔθετο. Strong: 1 pers. sing. praes. ind. act. skr. *dádhāmi*, gr. τίθημι; gr. θωμός, heap, goth. *dōms*, judgment.

The root **sē-*, to throw. Weak: lat. *satus*; gr. ἑτός. Strong: gr. ἵημι, lat. *sēvi*, *sēmen*; gr. ἀφέωκα, goth. *saíso*.

III. *ā*-series.

The root **sthā-*, to stand. Weak: ved. *savyeṣṭhā́* (*savyeṣṭhár-*), the warrior, who stands on the left of the charioteer; part. perf. pass. skr. *sthitá-s*, gr. στατός. Strong: 1 pers. sing. praes. ind. act. skr. *tíṣṭhāmi*, gr. ἵστημι.

The root **āĝ-*, to drive. Weak: ved. *jmán-*, path, way; 1 pers. sing. praes. ind. act. (originally **aĝó*) skr. *ájāmi*, gr. *ἄγω*, lat. *agō*. Strong: skr. *ājí-ṣ*, race, contest, gr. *στρατηγός*, lat. *ambāges*; gr. *ἀγωγή*.

IV. *ō*-series.

The root **dō-*, to give. Weak: skr. part. perf. pass. *ā-tta-s*, taken away; ved. *devá-tta-s*, given by a god; gr. *δάνος*, lat. *datus*, *dator*; gr. *δοτός*. Strong: 1 pers. sing. praes. ind. act. skr. *dádāmi*, gr. *δίδωμι*, lat. *dōnum*.

The root **ōd-*, to smell. Weak: gr. *ὄζω*, *ὀδμή*, lat. *odor*, *oleo*. Strong: gr. *ὄδωδα*, *εὐώδης*.

Cf. Brugmann 1, 250 sqq., who differs in many points from the exposition given above.

It can not be denied, that it is very difficult to distinguish the *ē*-series from the *ā*-series, cf. skr. *cáru-*, gladsome, pleasant: lat. *cārus*, goth. *hōrs*; ohg. *stēm*, *stām*: gr. *ἵστημι* (dor. *ἵσταμι*), skr. *tiṣṭhāmi* &c.

§ 7. **Idg. a.** The idg. *a* is represented in Aryan by *a*. Tautosyllabic *ai̯*, *au̯* were contracted in Sanskrit to *e*, *o*.

idg. **aĝó*: skr. *ájāmi* (for **ajámi*, **ajá*), I drive, gr. *ἄγω*, lat. *agō*, icel. inf. *aka*.

idg. **aĝró-s*: ved. *ájra-s*, field, plain, gr. *ἀγρός*, lat. *ager*, goth. *akrs*.

idg. **aks-*: skr. *ákṣa-s*, axle, gr. *ἄξων*, lat. *axis*, ohg. *ahsa*.

idg. **aḱró-s*: skr. *-açra-*, angle (angular), gr. *ἄκρος*, cf. lat. *ācer* (**áḱro-s*) and ved. *áçmā* (*n*), stone, gr. *ἄκμων*.

idg. **áñĝhos*: ved. *áṁhas*, distress, lat. *angus-* in *angustus*, cf. ved. *aṁhú-*, narrow, goth. *aggwus* and also gr. *ἄγχω*, lat. *angō*, gr. *ἄγχι*, *ἀγχοῦ* &c.

idg. **anə-*, **ane-*: skr. *ániti*, he breathes, *anilá-s*, wind, gr. *ἄνεμος*, lat. *animus*, *anima*, goth. praet. *uzōn*, expired.

idg. **anti*: ved. *ánti*, opposite, before, gr. *ἀντί*, lat. *ante*, goth. *and*.

idg. **apo*: skr. *ápa*, away, forth, off, gr. *ἀπό*, goth. *af*.

idg. **arĝ-*: skr. *árjuna-s*, white, ved. *rajatá-s*, silvery, skr. *rajatá-m*, silver (perhaps idg. **raĝ-* by the side of **arĝ-*; Avestian has *ĕrĕzata-*, silver), gr. *ἄργυρος*, lat. *argentum*.

idg. **ĝhans-*: skr. *haṁsá-s*, goose, swan, gr. *χήν*, lat. *anser* (**hanser*), ohg. *gans*.

idg. **i̯aĝ-* (weak form of **i̯āĝ-*): skr. *yájāmi* (for **yajámi*, idg. **i̯aĝṓ*), I worship, gr. *ἅζομαι* (**i̯aĝ-i̯o-mai̯*), cf. skr. *yajñá-s*, worship, sacrifice, gr. *ἁγνός* (idg. **i̯aĝnó-s*), ved. *yajás*, worship, gr. *ἅγος* (idg. **i̯aĝos*), ved. *yajya-*, venerable, gr. *ἅγιος* (idg. **i̯aĝi̯o-s*, **i̯aĝii̯o-s*).

idg. **kakud-*, **kakūd-*: skr. *kakút* (*d*), *kakúdmān* (*nt*), top, summit, lat. *cacūmen* (**cacūdmen*).

idg. **kark-*: skr. *karká-s*, *karkaṭa-s*, crab, gr. *καρκίνος*, lat. *cancer* (**carcer* or **carcen*?)

idg. **mad-*: ved. *mádāmi* (**madámi*), I am drunk, gr. *μαδάω*, lat. *madeō* (see Zubatý, Archiv f. Slav. phil. 13, 418 sqq.).

idg. **skandṓ*: skr. *skándāmi* (**skandámi*), I spring, lat. *scandō*.

Heterosyllabic *ai̯*, *au̯*:

idg. **sai̯ó-*: ved. *sayatvá-m*, tie, from the root **sāi̯-*, **sai̯-*, see below.

idg. **au̯ṓ*: skr. *ávāmi* (**avámi*), I help, I protect, cf. lat. *aveō*.

Tautosyllabic *ai̯*, *au̯*, contracted to *e*, *o*:

idg. **ai̯dh-*: skr. *édhas*, fuel, gr. *αἴθω*, lat. *aedes*, also ohg. *eit*, ags. *ād*, funeral pile.

idg. **sai̯-* (weak form of **sāi̯-*): skr. *sétu-ṣ*, joining, dam, bridge, ved. *setár-*, who binds, lat. *saeta*, bristle, ohg. *seid*, ags. *sāda*, snare, string.

idg. **au̯g*-: skr. *ójas*, ved. *ojmán*-, strength, power, lat. *augustus*, *augmentum*, *augeō*, goth. *aukan*, cf. gr. *αὐξάνω*, lat. *auxilium*.

§ 8. **Idg. ā.** Idg. *ā* = skr. *ā*:

idg. **āĝi-s*: skr. *ājí-ṣ*, race, contest, cf. gr. *στρατηγός* (*στρατᾱγός*) and skr. *samāja-s*, meeting, company. A weak form of the root is found in skr. *ájāmi*, gr. *ἄγω*, lat. *agō*, icel. inf. *aka*.

idg. **i̯āĝo-s*: skr. -*yāja*-, sacrifice (*yāga*- has got *g* by analogy), cf. skr. *yájāmi*, avest. *yazāmi*, gr. *ἅζομαι*.

idg. **bhāĝhu-s*: skr. *bāhú-ṣ*, arm, gr. *πῆχυς*, dor. *πᾶχυς*, ohg. *buog*.

idg. **bhrā́ter*-: skr. *bhrā́tā* (*r*), gr. *Φρά̄τηρ*, lat. *frāter*, goth. *brōþar*.

idg. **māter*-: skr. *mātā́*, gr. *μήτηρ*, dor. *μά̄τηρ*, lat. *māter*, ohg. *muoter*.

idg. **sthā*-: skr. *tíṣṭhāmi*, I stand, gr. *ἵστημι*, dor. *ἵστᾱμι*, lat. *stāre*.

idg. **éḱu̯ā*: skr. *áçvā*, mare, lat. *equa*.

Heterosyllabic *āi̯*, *āu̯*:

idg. **sāi̯o*-: skr. *sāyá-m*, evening, if it belongs to **sāi̯*-, **sai̯*-, to bind, to fasten, to loosen (for the signification cf. gr. *βουλῡτόνδε*).

idg. **dāu̯o*-: skr. *dāvá*-, burning, fire, cf. gr. *δήϊος*, *δέδηε*. Weaker forms of this root are contained in gr. *δαίω* (idg. **dau̯i̯ō*), skr. *dunómi*, I burn, I torture (idg. **dunéu̯mi*).

idg. **nā́u̯m̥*: skr. acc. sing. *nā́vam*, ship, gr. *νῆα*, lat. *nāvem*, cf. icel. dat. *nói*.

Tautosyllabic *āi̯*, *āu̯*:

idg. -*āi̯*: ved. dat. sing. fem. *suvapatyāí*, to her who has good offspring, gr. *χώρᾳ*, olat. *Mātūtā*, goth. *gibai*.

idg. *nā́u̯-s: skr. nā́u-ṣ, ship, gr. ναῦς, cf. icel. naust.

§ 9. **Idg. e.** The idg. *e* became *a* before the separation of Indian and Iranian and fell together with the idg. *a* (see § 7) and *o* (see § 11). This change took place after the palatalization of gutturals: see § 53.

idg. *ésti: skr. ásti, is, gr. ἔστι, lat. est, goth. ist.

idg. *é-bherom: skr. ábharam, I bore, gr. ἔφερον.

idg. *bhérō: skr. bhárāmi, I bear, gr. φέρω, lat. ferō, goth. baíra.

idg. *ĝénos, *ĝénes-: ved. jánas, family, race, gr. γένος (gen. γένεος), lat. genus (gen. generis).

idg. *g̑hen-: skr. hánmi, I beat, I kill, gr. θείνω.

idg. *g̑héros: ved. háras, heat, gr. θέρος.

idg. *nébhos: skr. nábhas, cloud, sky, gr. νέφος, cf. gr. νεφέλη, lat. nebula, ohg. nebul.

idg. *pénqe: skr. páñca, five, gr. πέντε, lat. quinque, goth. fimf.

idg. *peq-: skr. pácāmi, I cook, gr. πέσσω, lat. coquō.

idg. *péri: skr. pári, around, gr. πέρι, goth. faír-.

idg. *pet-: skr. pátāmi, I fly, I fall, gr. πέτομαι, πίπτω, lat. petō.

idg. *qe: skr. ca, and, gr. τε, lat. que.

idg. *qeru-s: skr. carú-ṣ, kettle, pot, a certain offering-porridge, icel. hverr.

idg. *qetu̯óres: skr. catvā́ras, four, goth. fidwōr, cf. lat. quatuor and gr. τέσσαρες.

idg. *rég̑os, *rég̑es-: skr. rájas, atmosphere, mist, gloom, dust, darkness, goth. riqis, cf. gr. ἔρεβος (*ereg̑os).

idg. *séĝhos, *séĝhes-: skr. sáhas, strength, might, violence, goth. sigis, cf. skr. sáhāmi, I overpower, I withstand, gr. ἔχω.

idg. *u̯éĝhō: skr. váhāmi, I carry, gr. pamphyl. ϝέχω, lat. vehō, goth. -wiga.

idg. **u̯l̥qe*, **lúqe*: skr. *vŕ̥ka*, voc. wolf, gr. λύκε, cf. lat. *lupe* (only for the ending of the vocative; the word *lupus* is to be separated from λύκος). Goth. *wulf* has lost the *auslaut-e*.

idg. **bhérethe*, **bhérete*: skr. *bháratha*, you bear, gr. φέρετε, goth. *baíriþ*.

Heterosyllabic *ei̯*, *eu̯*:

idg. **qei̯-*: ved. *cáyate*, punishes, gr. arcad. τείω.

idg. **smei̯-*: skr. *smáyate*, smiles, cf. gr. μειδιάω, φιλομμειδής, engl. *smile*.

idg. **k̂léu̯os*: skr. *çrávas*, glory, fame, gr. κλέος.

Tautosyllabic *ei̯*, *eu̯* = skr. *e*, *o* (contracted from *ai̯*, *au̯*):

idg. **éi̯mi*: skr. *émi*, gr. εἶμι.

idg. **ĝhéi̯men-*: ved. *héman-*, winter, gr. χεῖμα, χειμών.

idg. **bhéu̯dhō*: skr. *bódhāmi*, I perceive, goth. *biuda*, cf. gr. πυνθάνομαι, πεύθομαι.

idg. **ĝeu̯ster-*: ved. *joṣṭár-*, *jóṣṭar-*, loving, cf. gr. γευστήριον, goblet, and skr. *juṣáte*, is glad, loves, gr. γεύω, lat. *gustus*, goth. *kiusan*, *kustus*.

§ 10. **Idg. ē.** The idg. *ē* became *ā* before the end of the Aryan period, but after the palatalization of gutturals (see § 53). So it fell together with the idg. *ā* (see § 8) and *ō* (see § 12).

idg. **ēd-*: skr. (Pāṇini) *ā́da*, have (has) eaten, *ādivā́n* (*ṁs*), having eaten, gr. ἐδηδώς, lat. *ēdimus*, goth. *ētum*.

idg. **ḗsm̥*: skr. *ā́sam*, I was, gr. hom. ἦα.

idg. **dhē-*: skr. *dádhāmi*, I put, gr. τίθημι.

idg. **ĝēni-*: skr. *-jāni-*, wife, goth. *qēns*.

idg. **plē-*: ved. *prātá-*, *prāṇa-*, full, gr. πλήρης, lat. *plēnus*, *-plētus*.

idg. **rēĝ-*: skr. *rā́j-* (nom. *rā́ṭ* instead of **rāk*, idg. **rēks*), king, lat. *rēx*, gall. *-rīx* (goth. *reiks* is of Celtic origin).

idg. **uéti*: skr. *váti*, blows, gr. ἄησι (*əuéti), cf. goth. *waian*.

idg. **dusmenēs*: skr. *durmanās*, dejected, gr. δυσμενής.

idg. **siēs*, **siiēs*: skr. *syās* (*siyās*), thou mayst be, lat. *siēs*, cf. gr. εἴης (**es-iēs* for **s-iēs*).

idg. **mātē(r)*: skr. *mātá*, mother, gr. μήτηρ, lat. *māter*, ohg. *muoter*. The *-ter-* stems in Lithuanian have the nominative in *-tė*; so lith. *motė*, wife, = skr. *mātá*.

Heterosyllabic *ēi*, *ēu*:

idg. **uēiu-s*: skr. *vāyú-ṣ*, wind, air, cf. *váti*, gr. ἄησι.

idg. **dhēuō*: skr. *dhávāmi*, I run, cf. gr. θέω.

Tautosyllabic *ēi*, *ēu*:

idg. **é-dēiksm̥*: skr. **ádāikṣam*, I showed, gr. ἔδειξα.

idg. **diēu-s*: skr. *dyáu-ṣ*, heaven, gr. Ζεύς.

§ 11. **Idg. o.** The idg. *o* became *a* before the separation of Indian and Iranian and fell together with the idg. *a* (see § 7) and *e* (see § 9). Cf. however P. B. Beitr. 22, 546, where I have suggested a restriction of this rule.

idg. **októu*, **oktō*: skr. *aṣṭáu*, ved. *aṣṭá*, eight, gr. ὀκτώ, lat. *octō*, goth. *ahtau*.

idg. **opos*: ved. *ápas*, work, lat. *opus*.

idg. **osth-*: skr. *ásthi*, bone, gr. ὀστέον, lat. *os* (gen. *ossis* from **osthes*, see Zubatý, Kuhn's Zeitschr. 31, 6).

idg. **bhéronti*: skr. *bháranti*, they bear, gr. φέρουσι, dor. φέροντι.

idg. **dedórke*: skr. *dadárça*, has seen, gr. δέδορκε.

idg. **dorkéiō*: skr. *darçáyāmi*, I let see, I show, goth. *gatarhja*.

idg. **dómo-s*, **domu-s*: ved. *dáma-s*, house, gr. δόμος, lat. *domus*.

idg. **ĝeĝóna*: skr. *jajàna*, I produced, gr. γέγονα.

idg. **ghono-s*: skr. *ghaná-s*, slayer (ved.), compact, compacted mass, cloud, gr. φόνος, cf. skr. *hánmi*, gr. θείνω.

idg. **koksā*: skr. *kakṣā* (*kákṣa-s*), region of the girth, girdle, cincture, circular wall, enclosed court, lat. *coxa*, mhg. *hahse*.

idg. **qotero-s*: skr. *katará-s*, who (from two), gr. πότερος, ion. κότερος, cf. goth. *hwaþar*.

idg. **moni-s*: skr. *maṇí-ṣ*, jewel (though Vedic, this word must be a prācritism; genuine-skr. would be **mani-ṣ*), os. *meni*, cf. lat. *monīle*.

idg. **póti-s*: skr. *páti-ṣ*, lord, husband, gr. πόσις, goth. *-faþs*, cf. the feminine idg. **pótnī* (gen. **potnii̯ēs* or **potnii̯ās*): skr. *pátnī*, lady, mistress, wife, gr. πότνια.

idg. **próti*: skr. *práti*, against, gr. προτί (πρός).

idg. **rótho-s*, **rothā*: skr. *rátha-s*, chariot, lat. *rota*, ohg. *rad*. Cf. also gr. ῥόθος, which allows however an other explication.

idg. **ul̥qo-s*, **lúqo-s*: skr: *vṛka-s*, wolf, gr. λύκος, goth. *wulfs*.

idg. **é-bhereto*: skr. *ábharata*, gr. ἐφέρετο, 3 pers. sing. imperf. med. from the root **bher-*, to bear.

Heterosyllabic *oi̯*, *ou̯*:

idg. **du̯oi̯ó-s*: skr. *dvayá-s*, double, gr. δοιός.

idg. **óu̯i-s*: skr. *ávi-ṣ*, sheep, gr. ὄϊς, οἶς, lat. *ovis*, ohg. *awi*.

Tautosyllabic *oi̯*, *ou̯* = skr. *e*, *o* (contracted from *ai̯*, *au̯*):

idg. **lelói̯qa*: skr. *riréca*, I left, gr. λέλοιπα, goth. *laihw*.

idg. **u̯ói̯da*: skr. *véda*, I know, gr. οἶδα, goth. *wait*.

idg. **bhéroi̯s*: skr. *bháreṣ*, thou mayst bear, gr. φέροις, goth. *bairais*.

idg. **bhebhóu̯dha*: skr. *bubódha*, I perceived, cf. goth. *bauþ*.

idg. **sūnóu̯s*: skr. *sūnóṣ*, goth. *sunaus*, gen. of skr. *sūnú-ṣ*, son, goth. *sunus*.

I can not agree with Brugmann (Kuhn's Zeitschr. 24, 1 sqq., Morphol. unters. 3, 91 sqq.), Osthoff (Morphol. unters. 1, 207 sqq. note, cf. 4, 303 note), Streitberg (Idg. forschungen 3,

364 sqq.) and others, who suppose, that the idg. *o* in Aryan always became *ā* in open syllables. J. Schmidt (Kuhn's Zeitschr. 25, 1 sqq.) and Meillet (Mém. de la Soc. de Ling. 9, 142 sqq.) have proved, that the idg. *o* in open syllables generally is represented by *a*. The *ā* of skr. *jā́nu*, knee, must not be compared with the *o* of gr. *γόνυ*, but with the *ω* of gr. *γωνία* and skr. *dā́ru*, wood, is not identical with gr. *δόρυ*, but differs from it in the radical vowel (*ō* : *o*). So the *ā* of skr. *pā́dam*, *dātā́ram* does not correspond to the *o* of gr. *πόδα*, *δώτορα*, but to the *ō* of gr. dor. *πώς*, lat. *datōrem*. About the vocalisation of the causatives (skr. *svāpáyāmi* = lat. *sōpiō*) and iteratives (ved. *patáyāmi*, cf. gr. *ποτέομαι*) see not only Meillet, but also Delbrück, Idg. forschungen 4, 132 sq.

De Saussure 96 sq. and Bartholomae (Bezz. Beitr. 17, 93, 103) have made probable, that there was originally a difference between the *o* in the *e*-series and the *o*, which is weakened from *ō*: in Armenian *o* : *e* is represented by *o*, but *o* : *ō* has become *a*. In as early a period as the Aryan or Indo-Iranian these two *o*'s had fallen together.

§ 12. **Idg. ō.** The idg. *ō* became *ā* and fell together with the idg. *ā* (see § 8) and *ē* (see § 10). This transition took place in the same time as the change of *o* to *a*, i. e. in the Aryan period (see § 11).

idg. **ōk̂ú-s*: skr. *āçú-ṣ*, swift, gr. *ὠκύς*, cf. lat. comp. *ōcior*.

idg. **ōmó-s*: skr. *āmá-s*, raw, gr. *ὠμός*.

idg. **dṓno-m*: skr. *dā́na-m*, gift, lat. *dōnum*, cf. idg. **didōti*, skr. *dádāti* (for **didāti*), gives, gr. *δίδωσι*.

idg. **u̯l̥qōd*: skr. *vŕ̥kād*, abl. of *vŕ̥ka-s*, wolf, cf. the Latin ablatives ending in *-ōd*, *-ō*.

idg. **bhéretōd*: ved. *bháratād*, must bear, gr. *φερέτω*, cf. lat. *fertō*.

idg. **su̯ésō(r)*: skr. *svásā (r)*, sister, lat. *soror*, goth. *swistar*, cf. gr. ἔορ· θυγάτηρ, ἀνεψιός.

idg. **bhérō*: skr. *bhárāmi (*bhárā)*, gr. φέρω, lat. *ferō*, goth. *baíra*.

Heterosyllabic *ōi̯*, *ōu̯*:

idg. **pōi̯u-*: ved. *pāyú-ṣ*, guarding, protecting, protector, gr. πῶυ. The root is **pōi̯-* (**pō-*: skr. *páti*, protects), **poi̯-* (gr. ποιμήν), **pī-* (ved. *-pīti-*).

idg. **dōu̯en-*, **dōmen-*: ved. inf. *dāváne*, *dā́mane*, to give, cf. gr. δοῦναι (δοϝέναι), δόμεναι.

Tautosyllabic *ōi̯*, *ōu̯* (of *ōi̯* no example):

idg. **g̑ōu̯-s*: skr. *gáu-ṣ*, cow, bull, gr. βοῦς, lat. *bōs* (**vōs*), ohg. *chuo*.

§ 13. **Idg. ə.** The idg. *ə* in general is represented in Aryan by *i*. So this Indo-Iranian *i* can be a weak form of *a* (idg. *e*) as well as of *ā* (idg. *ē*, *ā*, *ō*). The tautosyllabic vowel-combinations *əi̯*, *əu̯* had been contracted to *ī*, *ū* before the end of the Indogermanic period.

Examples of *ə* : *e* (Bartholomae):

idg. **anə-*, **ane-*: skr. *ánimi*, I breathe, *anilá-*, wind: gr. ἄνεμος.

idg. **bherə-tro-m*, **bhere-tro-m*: ved. *bharítra-m*, arm: gr. φέρετρον, lat. *feretrum*.

idg. **ĝenə-tō(r)*, **ĝene-tō(r)*: skr. *janitā́ (r)*; father: gr. γενέτωρ.

idg. **isə-ró-s*, **ise-ró-s*: ved. *iṣirá-s*, strong, lively, quick: gr. ἱερός.

Further also:

idg. **təmə-ró-s*: skr. *timirá-s*, dark: *támas*, darkness.

idg. **g̑hən-*: skr. *hinásmi*, *hiṁsāmi*, I hurt: *hánmi*, I slay.

Other instances of idg. *ə*, skr. *i*:

idg. **pəté(r)*: skr. *pitā́*, father, gr. πατήρ, lat. *pater*, goth. *fadar*.

idg. **sthətó-s*: skr. *sthitá-s*, standing, gr. στατός.

idg. **é-dəto*: skr. *ádita*, 3 pers. sing. aor. med. of *dádāmi*, cf. gr. ἔδοτο (idg. ə in δάνος).

De Saussure 150 thinks, that ə, when followed by *i̯* or *u̯*, is represented in Indian by *a*, but the inaccuracy of this opinion is clearly shown by Bechtel 250 sqq. This scholar supposes, that ə fell together with *a*, if it had got the stress before the Aryan change of ə to *i*.

Instances of such *a*'s are:

skr. *rátna-m*, riches, treasure (ved.), jewel, pearl: *rātí-ṣ*, gracious, grace, gift, *rā́-s* (*rāy-*), wealth, lat. *rēs*.

ved. *dátra-m*, gift: *dā́na-m*, *dádāmi*, gr. δῶρον, δίδωμι, lat. *dōnum*, *dōs*.

skr. *kṣatrá-m*, rule, dominion (ved.), nobility: gr. κτῆμα.

skr. *ni-dhána-m*, end, death, *dhána-m*, prize of the contest, booty (ved.), wealth, property, money: *dádhāmi*, I put, gr. τίθημι.

Before *y*:

skr. *dáyate*, parts, allots, takes part, sympathizes, *dayā́*, sympathy, compassion, gr. δαίομαι.

skr. *dháyati*, sucks, drinks: ved. *dhāyáse*, to suck, to nourish.

skr. *páyas*, sap, liquid (ved.), water, milk: *pātum*, to drink.

skr. *váyati*, weaves, *vayā́*, twig (ved.): *vāna-m*, subst. weaving.

skr. *vyáyati*, envelops: *-vyāna-*, subst. enveloping.

skr. *hváyati*, calls: *hvātum*, to call.

Bechtel's theory is not improbable, but there are some objections to be made:

1° *kṣatrá-* is oxytonon: so it does not agree with Bechtel's rule.

2° in not a single of the above-mentioned words it is certain, that we have to do with idg. ə. If *rátna-m* really belongs to the same root as *rātí-ṣ*, *rā́-s*, lat. *rēs*, which however seems to be **rēi̯-*, than it might be reduced as well to **retno-m* as to **rətno-m*, for *e* is also a weak form of *ē* (cf. θετός : τίθημι). So *dhána-m* may be an idg. **dheno-m*, *dátra-m* an idg. **dotro-m* (cf. δοτός : δίδωμι) &c.

In *stená-*, thief, *sénā*, army, &c. we have idg. *ai̯* (resp. *ei̯* or *oi̯*), for *əi̯* was contracted to *ī* before the end of the Indogermanic period.

The combinations ot *ə* with nasals and liquids (which existed in Indogermanic by the side of the sonant nasals and liquids), require a separate treatment.

In the combinations *əm*, *ən* the idg. *ə* is regularly represented by *i*:

idg. **səmó-s*: ved. *simá-s*, each, cf. *sama-s*, each, somebody (**sm̥mó-s*).

idg. **təmərό-s*: skr. *timirá-s*, dark, cf. *támas*, darkness.

idg. **bəmb-*: skr. *bímba-m*, *bímba-s*, disk, cf. gr. βέμβιξ.

idg. **g̑hən-*: skr. *hinásmi*, *hiṁsāmi*, I hurt, cf. *hánmi*, I slay.

I assume the combinations *ər*, *əl* in those cases, where others have supposed long sonant liquids. They remained unchanged during the Aryan period; in Iranian they became *ar*. In Sanskrit they were treated in a different way, according as they stood or stood not in the neighbourhood of a labial consonant or vowel.

If they were not preceded or followed by a labial, the idg. *ər*, *əl* became *ir* (*il*) before vowels, *īr* before consonants. In the immediate neighbourhood of labials we find *ur* (*ul*) before vowels, *ūr* before consonants.

Idg. *ər*, *əl* before vowels, not in the neighbourhood of labials, skr. *ir*:

idg. *$\acute{g}$əri-s: skr. *girí-ṣ*, mountain, cf. lith. *giria*, forest, oslav. *gora*, mountain.

idg. *$\acute{g}$ərṓ: skr. *girā́mi*, I devour, cf. oslav. *žirą*, I devour, gr. βάραθρον, δέρεθρον.

idg. *gəlés: skr. *girás*, gen. abl. sing. of *gī́r*, voice, cf. oslav. *glasŭ*, voice, icel. *kalla*, to call (idg. *gals-) &c. There are also forms with *r* (lith. *garsas*, lat. *garriō*; gr. γῆρυς) and so it is possible, that the original form of *girás* is *gərés.

idg. *kərṓ: skr. *kirā́mi*, I pour out, I strew.

idg. *tərṓ: ved. *tirā́mi*, cf. idg. *térō, skr. *tárāmi*, I cross, and gr. τείρω, τέρετρον.

idg. *tərn̥s: ved. *tirás*, through, cf. lat. *trans*.

Idg. *ər*, *əl* before consonants, not in the neighbourhood of labials, skr. *īr*:

idg. *$\hat{k}$ərs-: ved. *çīrṣán-*, skr. *çīrṣá-m*, head, cf. gr. κόρση, κόρρη and skr. *çíras* (idg. *$\hat{k}$əros), head, gr. κάρᾱ, κάρη (*$\hat{k}$ərā).

idg. *dəlghó-s: skr. *dīrghá-s*, long, cf. gr. δολιχός, ἐνδελεχής, lat. *indulgeō*.

idg. *gəl-s (perhaps *gər-s): skr. *gī́r*, voice.

Further a great number of passive participles as *gīrṇá-*: *girā́mi*, *kīrṇá-*: *kirā́mi* &c. It is a matter of course, that skr. *jīrṇá-*, worn out, old, must not be identified with lat. *grānum* (idg. *$\bar{g}$rāno-). The *ŭr* of ved. *juráti*, *jū́ryati*, decays, grows frail, and other verbs, where no labial is found, is not yet explained: probably these words are loans from a dialect, where *ər* became *ur* (*ūr*) in every condition or they have taken their *u* from other verbs, in which *u* was developed according to the rule (*sphuráti*).

On the other hand we should expect *ūr* instead of *īr* in ved. *īrmá-s*, arm, which with lat. *armus*, goth. *arms* goes back on idg. *ərmó-s (*m* is a labial!).

Idg. *ər*, *əl* before vowels, in the neighbourhood of labials, skr. *ur*:

idg. **u̯əren-*: ved. *úraṇa-s*, ram, lamb, cf. gr. ἀρνός, gen. of *ἀρήν.

idg. **pəlú-s*: skr. *purú-*, much, gr. πολύς (*παλύς), cf. goth. *filu*.

idg. **sphəró*: skr. *sphurā́mi*, I make a quick motion, I dart, I twitch, cf. gr. σπαίρω &c.

idg. **g̑ərú-s*: skr. *gurú-ṣ*, heavy, important, worthy of honor cf. gr. βαρύς, goth. *kaúrus* and also lat. *gravis*.

Idg. *ər*, *el* before consonants, in the neighbourhood of labials, skr. *ūr*:

idg. **u̯ərdhu̯ó-s*: skr. *ūrdhvá-s*, high, tending upwards, gr. dor. βορθό- (*ϝαρθϝό-), cf. gr. ὀρθός, lat. *arduus* (without *u̯* in the *anlaut*, idg. **ərdhu̯ó-s*).

idg. **u̯əlmí-s*: skr. *ūrmí-ṣ*, wave, ags. *wielm*, *wylm*, ohg. *walm*.

idg. **u̯əlnā́*: skr. *ū́rṇā*, wool, cf. goth. *wulla* (but lat. *lāna* = gr. λάχνη).

idg. **pəru̯o-s*: skr. *pū́rva-s*, first, cf. oslav. *prŭvŭ* (i. e. *prĭvŭ*) and with *m* goth. *fruma*.

idg. **pəlnó-s*: skr. *pūrṇá-s*, full, cf. goth. *fulls*. Lat. *plēnus* has idg. *ē* and corresponds to ved. *prāṇa-*.

idg. **pəl-s*: skr. *pū́r*, stronghold, fortified town, cf. gr. πόλις.

idg. **məldhen-*: skr. *mūrdhā́* (*n*), head, cf. ags. *molda*.

idg. **bhərĝo-s*: skr. *bhūrja-s* birch, cf. ohg. *pirihha*.

idg. **dəru̯ā*: skr. *dū́rvā*, millet-grass, dutch *tarwe*, wheat.

§ 14. **Idg. i.** Idg. *i* = skr. *i*.

idg. **imés*, **imén*: skr. *imás*, we go, gr. ἴμεν.

idg. **bhibhéi̯mi*: skr. *bibhémi*, I am afraid, ohg. *bibēm*.

idg. **diu̯í*: skr. *diví*, in heaven, gr. Διί.

idg. **i-d*: skr. *i-d-ám*, this, lat. *id*, goth. *it-a*.

idg. **u̯idmé*, **u̯idmén*: skr. *vidmá*, we know, gr. ἴδμεν, ἴσμεν, goth. *witum*.

idg. **óu̯i-s*: skr. *áviṣ*, sheep, gr. ὄϊς, οἶς, lat. *ovis*, goth. *awi-*.

idg. **su̯ādistho-s*: skr. *svā́diṣṭha-s*, sweetest, gr. ἥδιστος (*ᾱ̔διστος).

idg. **ésmi*: skr. *ásmi*, I am, gr. εἰμί, lesb. ἔμμι (*ἐσμι), goth. *im*.

idg. **esti*: skr. *ásti*, is, gr. ἔστι, lat. *est*, goth. *ist*.

idg. **idhi*: skr. *ihí* (**idhí*), go, gr. ἴθι.

§ 15. **Idg. i.** Idg. *ī* = skr. *ī*.

idg. **g̑īu̯ó-s*: skr. *jīvá-s*, living, lat. *vivus*, cf. gr. βίος, goth. *qius* (idg. **g̑iu̯o-s*).

idg. **grīu̯ā́*: skr. *grīvā́*, neck, oslav. *griva*, mane.

idg. **pī́u̯en-*: skr. *pī́vā* (*n*), fat, gr. πίων.

idg. **pī-*, weakest form of **pōi̯-*, to drink (not to confound with **pōi̯-*, to protect): skr. *pītá-s*, drunk, gr. πίνω, πῖθι, cf. skr. *pātum*, to drink, perf. *papā́u*, gr. πέπωκα, &c.

idg. **sīmén-* (root **sī-*, **sai̯-*, **sāi̯-*): skr. *sīmā́* (*n*), crown, border, frontier, limit, cf. gr. ἱμάς.

idg. **u̯īró-s*: skr. *vīrá-s*, man, hero, cf. lat. *vir*, goth. *waír* and gr. ἴς, ἶφι, lat. *vīs*. A stronger form of the root is contained in skr. *váyas*, strength, health, youth, age.

§ 16. **Idg. u.** Idg. *u* = skr. *u*:

Idg. **dhugətē(r)*: skr. *duhitā́* (*r*), daughter, cf. gr. θυγάτηρ and goth. *daúhtar*, lith. *duktė́*.

idg. **jugó-m*: skr. *yugá-m*, yoke, generation, an age of the world, gr. ζυγόν, lat. *jugum*, goth. *juk*.

idg. **k̑unós*: skr. *çúnas*, gr. κυνός, gen. of skr. *çvā́*, dog, gr. κύων.

idg. **k̑lutó-s*: skr. *çrutá-s*, heard, heard of, famed, gr. κλυτός, lat. *in-clutus* (cf. with *ū* ags. *hlúd*).

idg. **rudhəró-s*: skr. *rudhirá-s*, red, cf. gr. ἐρυθρός (idg. **erudhró-s*), lat. *ruber*. The root **reu̯dh-*, **ereu̯dh-* is a secondary formation from **ereu̯*, cf. skr. *aruṇá-s* and *aruṣá-s*, ruddy.

idg. **su̯ādú-s*: skr. *svādú-ṣ*, sweet, gr. ἡδύς.

idg. **nu*: skr. *nú*, now, gr. νύ, goth. *nu*.

I do not accept the theory, according to which idg. *ru* became *r̥*, when there was an *u* in the following syllable: *çr̥ṇóti*, hears, goes back on **k̑l̥-ne-u-ti* (root **k̑elu-*, cf. de Saussure 244, Pedersen, Idg. forschungen 2, 307).

§ 17. **Idg. ū.** Idg. *ū* = skr. *ū*:

idg. **bhūtí-s* (root **bhū-*, **bheu̯ə-*, **bheu̯e-*): skr. *bhūtí-ṣ*, being, prosperity, cf. gr. φύσις.

idg. **dhūmó-s*: skr. *dhūmá-s*, smoke, vapor, gr. θυμός, lat. *fūmus*.

idg. **k̑ūro-s*: skr. *çū́ra-s*, mighty, bold, hero, gr. -κῦρος in ἄ-κῦρος, not valid, cf. τὸ κῦρος, κύριος.

idg. **mū́s*: ved. *mū́ṣ-*, mouse, gr. μῦς, lat. *mūs*, ohg. *mūs*.

idg. **nū*: ved. *nū́*, now, gr. νῦν.

§ 18. **Idg. m̥.** The idg. *m̥* became *a* during the Aryan period; so it fell together with *n̥* (see § 19), *a* (see § 7), *e* (see § 9) and *o* (see § 11):

idg. **g̯m̥skhéti*: skr. *gácchati*, goes, cf. gr. imperat. βάσκε. The root is **g̯em-*.

idg. **g̯m̥tó-s*: skr. *gatá-s*, gone, gr. βατός, lat. *-ventus* and idg. **g̯m̥ti-s*: skr. *gáti-ṣ*, going, issue, refuge, gr. βάσις, goth. *-qumþi-* (root **g̯em-*).

idg. **k̑m̥tó-m*: skr. *çatá-m*, hundred, gr. ἑ-κατόν, lat. *centum*, goth. *hund*. That we have to do with *m̥*, appears from lith. *szimtas*.

idg. **dék̑m̥*: skr. *dáça*, gr. δέκα, lat. *decem*, goth. *taihun*. Notice the *m* of lith. *deszimt*.

Before *i̯*, *u̯* and before vowels we find *m̥m*:

idg. **g̑m̥mi̯ē̆t*: ved. *gamyā́t* must go (root **g̑em-*).

idg. **g̑eg̑m̥mu̯ṓs*: ved. *jaganvā́n* (*ṁs*), with *nv* from *mv* (see § 37), part. perf. act. from **g̑em-*, to go.

idg. **sm̥mó-s*: ved. *sama-s*, somebody, gr. ἀμό-, goth. *sums*, cf. **səmó-s*, ved. *simá-s* each (this word has been explained differently by Geldner, Ved. studien 2, 188 sqq.).

idg. **sm̥mer-*: skr. *sámā* (*ā*-stem), half a year, year, ags. *sumor*, engl. *summer*.

§ 19. **Idg. n̥.** The dental, guttural and palatal *n̥* are represented in Aryan by *a*. They have fallen together with *m̥* (see § 18), *a* (see § 7), *e* (see § 9) and *o* (see § 11).

Instances of the dental *n̥*:

idg. **n̥-mr̥to-s*: skr. *amṛ́ta-*, immortal, gr. ἄμβροτος.

idg. **mn̥tó-s*: skr. *matá-s*, thought, gr. -ματος in αὐτόματος, lat. *-mentus*, goth. *munds*.

idg. **néu̯n̥*: skr. *náva*, cf. gr. ἐννέα. Lat. *novem* has borrowed its *m* from *decem*, but goth. *niun* is entirely identical with skr. *náva*. Lith. *devyni* proves, that the original form had *n̥* (not *m̥*).

Before *i̯*, *u̯* and before vowels we find *n̥n*:

idg. **mn̥ni̯etai̯*: skr. *mányate*, thinks, gr. μαίνεται.

idg. **g̑heg̑hn̥nu̯ṓs*: skr. *jaghanvā́n* (*ṁs*), part. perf. act. from **g̑hen-*, to slay.

idg. **tn̥nu̯ī́*: skr. *tanvī́*, fem. of *tanú-ṣ*, thin, cf. gr. τανυ-, lat. *tenuis*, obg. *dunni*.

idg. **n̥n-udro-s*: ved. *anudrá-*, waterless, gr. ἄνυδρος.

idg. **tn̥nú-s*: skr. *tanú-ṣ*, thin, see above.

Skr. *sánti*, they are, is not idg. **sn̥ti*, but **sénti* (Streitberg, Idg. forschungen 1, 82 sqq.).

An instance of the guttural *n̥* is:

idg. **l̥n̥ghú-s*: skr. *laghú-ṣ*, light, swift, insignificant, gr. ἐλαχύς (**el̥n̥ghú-s*), cf. ἐλαφρός (**el̥n̥ghró-s*) and goth. *leihts*. Lat. *levis* seems never to have contained a nasal.

Of the palatal *n̥*:

idg. **dn̥k̑éti*: skr. *dáçati*, bites, cf. gr. δάκνω, ἔδακον.

§ 20. **The problem of the long sonant nasals.** De Saussure 239 sqq., Brugmann 1, 208 sq. and others attribute long sonant nasals to the mother-language. In the same way they assume idg. *r̥̄*, *l̥̄*, which I have replaced by *ər*, *əl* (see § 13). These are represented in Sanskrit by *ir*, *il* (*ur*; *īr*, *ūr*) and stand on a level with idg. *əm*, *ən*, skr. *im*, *in*. Brugmann thinks, that those hypothetical *m̥̄*, *n̥̄* became *ā* in Aryan. but the cases, in which such *ā*'s are supposed, admit other explications, which seem more acceptable.

The aorist-forms skr. *ágām*, *ágās*, *ágāt* &c., which doubtlessly are identical with gr. ἔβην, ἔβης, ἔβη, dor. ἔβᾱν, ἔβᾱς, ἔβᾱ, are not derived from the root **gem-*, but from its synonyme **gā-* (see Persson, Studien zur lehre der wurzelerweiterung und wurzelvariation, Upsala 1891, 70). The *ā* of skr. *ágām*, gr. dor. ἔβᾱν is an idg. *ā* (not *m̥̄*) and the original paradigm was **égām*, **égās*, **égāt* &c. In a similar way are to be explained *sātá-*: *sanómi*, *vātá-*: *vanómi*, *ghāta-* (and *ghāti-*): *hánmi* and some other cases. But *jātá-*, born, seems to have taken its *j* instead of *jñ* by the influence of *jánati*, *janáyati*, *jajā́na* &c. The regular form **jñāta-* (idg. **ĝnātó-*) corresponds to lat. *-gnātus*, gall. *-gnātus*.

The *j* of the praesens *jā́yate* has the same origin as that of *jātá-* (*tāyáte*: *tanóti*, *khāyate*: *khánati* have been formed after the type of *jā́yate*). The substitution of *j* for *jñ* in *jātá-*, *jā́yate* is Indo-Iranian, cf. pers. *zād*, birth, *zādan*, to bear, to be born. In skr. *jānā́mi*, I know (= pers. *dānam*) we may explain the *j* instead of *jñ* by dissimilation (**jñānāmi*), cf. gr. γιγνώσκω, lat. *-gnōscō*.

If ved. *ātí-ṣ*, a waterbird, is to be compared with gr. νῆσσα, the following explanation seems possible: there was an *-i-* (*-ei̯-*, *-oi̯-*) stem **nā́ti-*, **n̥téi̯-* in the mother-language, which in Aryan became regularly **nā́ti-*, **atáï-*. Ved. *ātí-* is a contamination of **nā́ti-* and **atái̯-*. Lat. *anas*, ohg. *anut*, lith. *antis*, oslav. *ąty* are not clear (idg. **anat-*, **ant-*?). But perhaps it is preferable to separate *āti-* from νῆσσα (**nāti̯ā*) and to identify it with gr. ὠτίς (-ίδος), as has been proposed by Speyer (Museum 2, 435).

Unexplained are ved. *ā́ta-*, *ā́tā*, frame of a door: lat. *anta*; ved. *yā́tar-*, the wife of the husband's brother: gr. εἰνατέρες: lat. *janitrīces* &c. Von Bradke (Idg. forschungen 4, 87 sqq.) compares skr. *jārá-*, lover, paramour, with *jā́mātar-*, son in law, gr. γαμβρός, which combination from a semantic point of view would not seem very probable. Less credible yet is his etymology of skr. *dārá-*, wife (: gr. δάμαρ, 85 sqq.), for Johansson (Idg. forschungen 3, 229 sqq.) has shown its identity with gr. δῶλος (: δοῦλος).

§ 21. **Idg. r̥, l̥.** The idg. *r̥* and *l̥* are represented by *r̥*. Skr. *kl̥ptá-*, put in order, arranged, the only word that contains *l̥*, is a prācritism for **kr̥ptá-* (the etymology of *kalp-* is to be found in my Etym. wörterbuch der gotischen sprache, Amsterdam 1896, s. v. *halbs*).

Idg. *r̥* = skr. *r̥*:

idg. **ŕ̥kþo-s*: skr. *ŕ̥kṣa-s*, bear, gr. ἄρκτος, lat. *ursus*.

idg. **r̥néu̯mi*, **r̥numai̯*: ved. *r̥ṇómi*, I rise, I go, I attain, gr. ὄρνυμι (see Schmidt, Kuhn's Zeitschr. 32, 376 sqq.), ἄρνυμαι.

idg. **r̥sen-*: skr. *r̥ṣa-bhá-s*, bull, gr. ἄρσην, ἄρρην.

idg. *_dhr̥sné̯umi_: skr. _dhr̥ṣṇómi_, I dare, cf. gr. θρασύς, θαρρέω, goth. _gadaúrsan_.

idg. *_kr̥p-_: ved. _kŕ̥p-_, appearance, form, shape, lat. _corpus_.

idg. _mr̥nā́mi_, *_mr̥namai̯_: ved. _mr̥ṇā́mi_, I crush, gr. μάρναμαι.

idg. *_mr̥tó-s_: skr. _mr̥tá-s_, dead, ohg. _mord_, cf. skr. _mr̥tyú-ṣ_, _mr̥ti-ṣ_, death, lat. _mors_ and skr. _mriyáte_, dies, lat. _morior_.

idg. *_pr̥k̑skhéti_: skr. _pr̥cchá́ti_, asks, lat. _poscit_, cf. ohg. _forscōn_.

Idg. _l̥_ = skr. _r̥_:

idg. *_pl̥thú-s_: skr. _pr̥thú-ṣ_, wide, broad, gr. πλατύς, cf. lith. _platus_. The original forms of the stem were *_plóthu-_ (*_plótu-_) and *_pl̥thé̯u-_ (*_pl̥té̯u-_).

idg. *_u̯ĺ̥qo-s_: skr. _vŕ̥ka-s_, wolf, goth. _wulfs_, cf. idg. *_lúqo-s_, gr. λύκος.

idg. *_ĺ̥k̑i̯o-s_: skr. _ŕ̥çya-s_, the male of an antilope, cf. ags. _eolh_, ohg. _elaho_ and icel. _elgr_, lat. _alces_, russ. _losĭ_ (also lith. _elnis_, oslav. _jelenĭ_, armen. _eλn_).

About skr. _mriyáte_, dies, _kriyáte_, is being made, see Brugmann 1, 113. 233. About skr. _ir_, _īr_, _ur_, _ūr_ see § 13.

B. The relation of the Indian vowels to the Indogermanic.

§ 22. **The Indian vowels in general.** The Indian vocalism is distinguished from the Indogermanic by a far greater simplicity. Already in the Aryan period _ə_ in general was changed to _i_ and _e_, _o_, _m̥_, _n̥_ had fallen together with _a_, according to which _ē_, _ō_, _ā_ were represented only by _ā_. Afterwards, during the separate life of Indian, _ai̯_ (idg. _ai̯_, _ei̯_, _oi̯_) and _au̯_ (idg. _au̯_, _eu̯_, _ou̯_) were contracted to _e_ and _o_.

Hence it follows, that the *ā*-, *ē*- and *ō*-series had fallen together (weak: —, *i*, *a*. strong: *ā*). So there are in Indian but two vowel-series:

I. *a*-series (idg. *e*-series).

	Weak:	Strong:	Lengthened:
A.	— , *i*.	*a*.	*ā*.
B.	*y* (*i*), *ī*.	*e* (*ya*).	*āi* (*yā*).
C.	*v* (*u*), *ū*.	*o* (*va*).	*āu* (*vā*).
D.	*m* (*a*, *am*), *im*.	*am* (*ma*).	*ām* (*mā*).
E.	*n* (*a*, *an*), *in*.	*an* (*na*).	*ān* (*nā*).
F.	*r* (*ṛ*), *ĭr* (*ŭr*).	*ar* (*ra*).	*ār* (*rā*).
G.	*l* (*ṛ*), *ĭr* (*ŭr*).	*al* (*la*).	*āl* (*lā*).

II. *ā*-series (idg. *ē*-, *ā*-, *ō*-series).

	Weak:	Strong:
A.	— , *i*, *a*.	*ā*.
B.	*y* (*i*), *ī*, *e* (*ya*).	*āi* (*yā*).
C.	*v* (*u*), *ū*, *o* (*va*).	*āu* (*vā*).

According to the ancient Indian grammarians there was but one vowel-series. They considered *i*, *u*, *ṛ* (*ḷ*) as primitive vowels, which could be strengthened by a prefixed *a*-element. This strengthening was called *guṇa*. A second strengthening was produced by the further prefixion of *a* to the *guṇa*-vowel: the name of this increment was *vṛddhi*. It is to be noticed, that *a* is its own *guṇa*: *ā* is the corresponding *vṛddhi*.

So their vowel-system is as follows:

Simple vowels:	(*a*)	*i* (*ī*)	*u* (*ū*)	*ṛ* (*ṝ*).
Guṇa-vowels:	*a*	*e*	*o*	*ar*.
Vṛddhi-vowels:	*ā*	*āi*	*āu*	*ār*.

The older European linguists adopted this system, but the researches of the last thirty years have shown its inaccuracy (cf. § 6). It is to be observed, that the lengthened degree (*ā, āi, āu, ām, ān, ār, āl*) has extended its original dominion by the vṛddhation of vowels in secondary derivates (see von Bradke, Zeitschr. d. D. Morgenl. Ges. 40, 361 sqq.). The commencement of this secondary vṛddhation dates back to the Indogermanic period (see Bechtel 175; Streitberg, Idg. forschungen 3, 379 sqq.; also my remarks on the mutual relation of goth. *hana*: **hōn*, P. B. Beitr. 22, 189 sq., 545 sqq.).

I. *a*-series (idg. *e*-series).

idg. **pet-*, to fly, to fall.

Weak: ved. 1 pers. sing. aor. act. *ápaptam*, 3 pers. plur. perf. act. *paptúr*. Strong: skr. 1 pers. sing. praes. act. *pátāmi*, ved. 1 pers. sing. ind. iterat. act. *patáyāmi*. Lengthened: ved. 3 pers. sing. aor. pass. *ápāti*, skr. 1 pers. sing. praes. causat. act. *pātáyāmi*.

idg. **bheid-*, to split.

Weak: skr. part. perf. pass. *bhinná-s*, 3 pers. sing. praes. pass. *bhidyáte*; ved. *vibhī́daka-s*, Terminalia Bellerica (the younger form *vibhī́taka-* seems to be a loan from the Pāiçāci-dialect). Strong: skr. 1 pers. sing. fut. act. *bhetsyā́mi*, 1 pers. 3 pers. sing. perf. act. *bibhéda*. Lengthened: skr. 3 pers. sing. aor. act. *ábhāitsīt*.

idg. **bheudh-*, to perceive.

Weak: skr. part. perf. pass. *buddhá-s*, 3 pers. sing. praes. pass. *budhyáte*. Strong: skr. 1 pers. sing. praes. act. *bódhāmi*, 1 pers. 3 pers. sing. perf. act. *bubódha*. Lengthened: skr. 3 pers. sing. aor. act. **ábhāutsīt*.

idg. **gem-*, to go.

Weak: skr. 3 pers. plur. perf. act. *jagmúr*; part. perf. pass. *gatá-s*, 1 pers. sing. praes. act. *gácchāmi* (**gacchámi*), ved. 1 pers. sing. praes. act. *gámāmi* (**gamámi*). Strong: skr. 1 pers. sing. fut. act. *gamiṣyámi*, 2 pers. sing. perf. act. *jagántha*. Lengthened: skr. 1 pers. 3 pers. sing. perf. act. *jagáma*, ved. 1 pers. sing. praes. causat. act. *gāmáyāmi*.

idg. **tem-*, to be dark.

Weak: skr. *timirá-s*, dark. Strong: skr. *támas*, darkness. Lengthened: skr. *tāmrá-s*, dark-red.

idg. **men-*, to think.

Weak: ved. 2 pers. dual. perf. med. *mamnáthe*; skr. part. perf. pass. *matá-s*, 3 pers. sing. praes. med. *mányate*. Strong: skr. 3 pers. sing. fut. med. *maṁsyáte*. Lengthened: skr. 1 pers. sing. praes. causat. act. *mānáyāmi*.

idg. **bhendh-*, to bind.

Weak: skr. part. perf. pass. *baddhá-s*, 1 pers. sing. praes. act. *badhnámi*. Strong: skr. 1 pers. sing. fut. act *bandhiṣyámi*, 1 pers. 3 pers. sing. perf. act. *babándha*. Lengthened: skr. 3 pers. sing. aor. act. *ábhāntsīt*.

idg. **ter-*, to cross.

Weak: ved. part. praes. act. *títrat-*; 1 pers. sing. praes. act. *tirámi*, skr. part. perf. pass. *tīrṇá-s*. Strong: skr. 1 pers. sing. praes. act. *tárāmi*, 1 pers. sing. perf. act. *tatára*. Lengthened: skr. 3 pers. sing. aor. act. *átārṣīt*, 1 pers. 3 pers. sing. perf. act. *tatára*.

idg. **bher-*, to bear.

Weak: skr. 1 pers. 3 pers. sing. perf. med. *babhré*; part. perf. pass. *bhṛtá-s*; 1 pers. sing. praes. desiderat. act. *búbhūrṣāmi*. Strong: skr. 1 pers. sing. praes. act. *bhárāmi*, *bíbharmi* (*bibhármi*, Ṛv.), 2 pers. sing. perf. act. *babhártha*. Lengthened: ved. 3 pers. sing aor. act. *ábhārṣīt*, skr. 1 pers. 3 pers. sing. perf. act. *babhára*.

II. *ā*-series (idg. *ē*-, *ā*-, *ō*-series).

idg. **dhē-*, to put.

Weak: skr. 3 pers. sing. praes. med. *dhatté*; ved. part. perf. pass. *-dhita-s*; skr. *dhána-m*, prize of the contest, booty (ved.), wealth, money. Strong: skr. 1 pers. sing. praes act. *dádhāmi*, 1 pers. 3 pers. sing. perf. act. *dadháu.*

idg. **sthā-*, to stand.

Weak: skr. 1 pers. 3 pers. sing. perf. med. *tasthé*; part. perf. pass. *sthitá-s*. Strong: skr. 1 pers. sing. praes. act. *tíṣṭhāmi*, 1 pers. 3 pers. sing. perf. act. *tasthâu.*

idg. **dō-*, to give.

Weak: skr. 3 pers. sing. praes. med. *dátte*; ved. part. perf. pass. *-dita-s*. Strong: skr. 1 pers. sing. praes. act. *dádāmi*, 1 pers. 3 pers. sing. perf. act. *dadáu.*

idg. **nāi̯-* (**nēi̯? *nōi̯?*), to lead.

Weak: skr. 1 pers. 3 pers. sing. perf. med. *ninyé*; ved. 1 pers. plur. perf. act. *ninimá*; skr. part. perf. pass. *nītá-s*; 1 pers. sing. praes. act. *náyāmi*, 1 pers. sing. fut. act. *neṣyā́mi*. Strong: skr. 1 pers. sing. praes. causat. act. *nāyáyāmi.*

idg. **dāu̯-*, to burn.

Weak: skr. 1 pers. sing. praes. act. *dunómi*; part. perf. pass. *dūná-s*; *dava-s*, fire, burning. Strong: skr. 1 pers. sing. praes. causat. act. *dāváyāmi.*

The Indogermanic mother-language had also dissyllabic roots, a great part of which contained the combinations *ei̯e*, *eu̯e*, *eme*, *ene*, *ere*, *ele*. In Indian these *udātta*-roots are found only in a weaker form, with *ayi*, *avi*, *ami*, *ani*, *ari*, *ali*, i. e. idg. *ei̯ə*, *eu̯ə*, *emə*, *enə*, *erə*, *elə*. Such roots, which make part of the idg. *e*-series, are not easily to distinguish from the idg. *ē*-, *ā*- and *ō*-roots. Here it will be sufficient to refer to de Saussure 239 sqq.; Brugmann 1, 104 sqq.; Kretschmer, Kuhn's

Zeitschr. 31, 386 sq.; Bartholomae, Bezz. Beitr. 17, 109 sqq.; Hirt, Idg. forschungen 7, 185 sqq.

§ 23. **Skr. a.** In skr. *a* have fallen together the idg. vowels *a, e, o, m̥, n̥*.

Skr. *a* = idg. *a*:

skr. *ájāmi*, I drive, gr. ἄγω, lat. *agō*, icel. inf. *aka*.

ved. *ájra-s*, field, gr. ἀγρός, lat. *ager*, goth. *akrs*.

skr. *skándāmi*, I spring, lat. *scandō*.

skr. *ámba*, vocat. of *ambā*, mother, cf. gr. vocatives as νύμφα, δέσποτα.

Skr. *a* = idg. *e*:

skr. *ásti*, is, gr. ἔστι, lat. *est*, goth. *ist*.

skr. *ábharam*, I bore, gr. ἔφερον.

ved. *jánas*, family, race, gr. γένος, lat. *genus*.

ved. *háras*, heat, gr. θέρος.

skr. *páñca*, five, gr. πέντε, lat. *quinque*, goth. *fimf*.

skr. *bháratha*, you bear, *ábharata*, you bore, gr. φέρετε, ἐφέρετε, goth. *baíriþ*.

Skr. *a* = idg. *o*:

ved. *ápas*, work, lat. *opus*.

skr. *ásthi*, bone, gr. ὀστέον, lat. *os*.

skr. *dadárça*, has seen, gr. δέδορκε.

skr. *kakṣā*, region of the girth, girdle, cincture, lat. *coxa*, mhg. *hahse*.

skr. *práti*, against, gr. πρός.

skr. *vṛ́ka-s*, wolf, gr. λύκος, goth. *wulfs*.

Skr. *a* = idg. *m̥*.

skr. *gatá-s*, gone, gr. βατός, lat. *-ventus*.

skr. *çatá-m*, hundred, gr. ἑ-κατόν, lat. *centum*, goth. *hund*.

skr. *ratá-s*, ceased, content, gr. ἐρατός, cf. skr. *rámate*, stops, ceases, rests, finds pleasure in something, gr. ἔραμαι, ἠρέμα, goth. *rimis*.

skr. *sámā*, half a year, year, ags. *sumor*.

Skr. *a* = idg. *ṇ̥*:

skr. *amṛ́ta-s*, immortal, gr. ἄμβροτος.

skr. *matá-s*, thought, gr. -ματος, lat. *-mentus*, goth. *munds*.

ved. *anudrá-s*, waterless, gr. ἄνυδρος.

skr. *jaghána-m*, the hinder parts, the buttocks, gr. κοχώνη (*καχώνη), cf. skr. *jáṅghā*, lower half of the leg, and goth. *gaggan*. The first *a* in *jaghána-m* represents the idg. guttural *ṇ̥*.

skr. *bahú-ṣ*, abundant, much, gr. παχύς, cf. skr. comp. *báṁhīyān* (*ṁs*). The *a* of *bahú-ṣ* goes back on idg. palatal *ṇ̥*.

Perhaps skr. *a* = idg. *ə*: see § 13.

§ 24. **Skr. ā.** By skr. *ā* are represented the idg. *ā*, *ē*, *ō*.

Skr. *ā* = idg. *ā*:

skr. *bāhú-ṣ*, arm, gr. πῆχυς, dor. πᾶχυς, ohg. *buog*.

skr. *mātā́*, mother, gr. μήτηρ, dor. μάτηρ, lat. *māter*, ohg. *muoter*.

skr. *tíṣṭhāmi*, I stand, gr. ἵστημι, dor. ἵσταμι, lat. *stāre*, cf. skr. *ásthāt*, stood, gr. ἔστη, dor. ἔστα.

skr. *áçvā*, mare, lat. *equa*.

Skr. *ā* = idg. *ē*:

skr. *ādivā́n*, having eaten, gr. ἐδηδώς.

skr. *-jāni-*, wife, goth. *qēns*.

skr. *vā́ti*, blows, gr. ἄησι, goth. *waian*.

skr. *durmanās*, dejected, gr. δυσμενής.

Skr. *ā* = idg. *ō*:

skr. *āçú-ṣ*, swift, gr. ὠκύς, lat. comp. *ōcior*.

skr. *āmá-s*, raw, gr. ὠμός.

skr. *dā́na-m*, gift, lat. *dōnum*.

ved. *bhāratād*, must bear, gr. φερέτω, cf. lat. *fertō*.

§ 25. **Skr. i.** Skr. *i* goes back on idg. *i* and *ə*.

Skr. *i* = idg. *i*:

skr. *imás*, we go, gr. ἴμεν.

skr. *diví*, in heaven, gr. Διί.

skr. *ávi-ṣ*, sheep, gr. ὄϊς, οἶς, lat. *ovis*, goth. *awi-*.

skr. *ásti*, is, gr. ἔστι, lat. *est*, goth. *ist*.

Skr. *i* = idg. *ə*.

skr. *pitá*, father, gr. πατήρ, lat. *pater*, goth. *fadar*.

skr. *sthitá-s*, standing, gr. στατός.

skr. *timirá-s*, dark: *támas*, darkness, cf. also *támisrā*, darkness, dark night, lat. *tenebrae*, middle-dutch *deemster*.

skr. *girí-ṣ*, mountain, cf. lith. *giria*, forest (with idg. *r̥*) and oslav. *gora*, mountain (with idg. *ə*, *a* or *o*).

§ 26. **Skr. ī.** In general the skr. *ī* corresponds to the idg. *ī*, but before *r* + cons. it nearly always goes back on *ə*.

Skr. *ī* = idg. *ī*:

skr. *jīvá-s*, living, lat. *vīvus*.

skr. *pī́vā* (*n*), fat, gr. πῖων.

skr. *sīmā́* (*n*), crown, border, frontier, gr. ἱμᾱ́ς (ντ).

Skr. *īr* before consonants = idg. *ər*, *əl*:

ved. *īrmá-s*, arm, lat. *armus*, goth. *arms*.

skr. *dīrghá-s*, long, cf. gr. δολιχός, ἐνδελεχής.

In cases as skr. *līḍhá-s*, licked, *nīḍá-s*, nest, *ī* is lengthened from *i* (see § 61 and § 63).

§ 27. **Skr. u.** In general the skr. *u* corresponds to the idg. *u*, but before *r* + vowel it often represents the idg. *ə*.

Skr. *u* = idg. *u*:

skr. *urú-ṣ*, wide, cf. gr. εὐρύς (idg. **éu̯ru-*, **uréu-*).

skr. *yugá-m*, yoke, age, gr. ζυγόν, lat. *jugum*, goth. *juk*.

skr. *çrutá-s*, heard, heard of, gr. κλυτός.

skr. *nú*, now, gr. νύ, goth. *nu*.

Skr. *ur* before vowels (in the neighbourhood of labial sounds) = idg. *ər*, *əl*:

skr. *purú-*, much, gr. *πολύς* (**παλύς*), cf. goth. *filu.*

skr. *gurú-ṣ*, heavy, important, worthy of honor, cf. gr. *βαρύς*, goth. *kaúrus.*

In ved. *úraṇa-s,* ram, lamb, *ur* goes back on idg. *u̯ər.*

§ 28. **Skr. ū.** In general the skr. *ū* corresponds to the idg. *ū*, but before *r* + cons. it nearly always represents the idg. *ə.*

Skr. *ū* = idg. *ū*:

skr. *dhūmá-s,* smoke, vapor, gr. *θῡμός*, lat. *fūmus.*

skr. *çū́ra-s*, mighty, bold, hero, gr. *-κῡρος* in *ἄκῡρος.*

ved. *mū́ṣ-*, mouse, gr. *μῦς*, lat. *mūs*, ohg. *mūs.*

Skr. *ūr* before consonants (in the neighbourhood of labial sounds) = idg. *ər, əl*:

skr. *pū́rva-s,* first, cf. oslav. *prŭvŭ* (*prĭvŭ*) and with *m* goth. *fruma.*

skr. *pū́r*, fortified town, cf. gr. *πόλις.*

skr. *mūrdhā́* (*n*), head, cf. ags. *molda.*

In skr. *ūrmí-ṣ*, wave (= ags. *wielm, wylm*, ohg. *walm*) and *ū́rṇā*, wool (cf. goth. *wulla* with *l̥*), *ūr* represents idg. *u̯əl*; in skr. *ūrdhvá-s*, high (cf. gr. *ὀρθός*, lat. *arduus*), *ūr* = idg. **u̯ər.*

In cases as skr. *ūḍhá-s,* carried, ved. *dū́ḍā́ç-*, not pious, *ū* is lengthened from *u* (see § 61 and § 63).

§ 29. **Skr. e.** In skr. *e* have fallen together the idg. tautosyllabic combinations *ai̯, ei̯, oi̯* (but in no case *əi̯*, for this diphthong was contracted to *ī* before the separation of the Indogermanic dialects).

Skr. *e* = idg. *ai̯*:

skr. *édhas,* fuel, cf. gr. *αἴθω*, lat. *aedes*, ohg. *eit.*

skr. *sétu-ṣ*, joining, dam, bridge, cf. lat. *saeta,* bristle, ohg. *seid,* snare.

Skr. *e* = idg. *ei̯*:

skr. *émi,* I go, gr. *εἶμι.*

ved. *héman-*, winter, gr. *χεῖμα*, *χειμών*.

Skr. *e* = idg. *oi̯*:

skr. *véda*, I know, gr. *οἶδα*, goth. *wait*.

skr. *bháreṣ*, you may bear, gr. *φέροις*, goth. *baírais*.

Skr. *ed*, *edh* sometimes corresponds to idg. *ezd*, *ezdh* (see § 63):

ved. *sedyā́t*, 3 pers. sing. optat. perf. from *sad-*, to sit, avest. *hazdyāþ*.

skr. *edhí*, 2 pers. sing. imperat. from *as-*, to be.

§ 30. **Skr. o.** In skr. *o* have fallen together the idg. tautosyllabic combinations *au̯*, *eu̯*, *ou̯* (but not *əu̯*, which was contracted to *ū* before the separation of the Indogermanic dialects).

Skr. *o* = idg. *au̯*:

ved. *ojmán-*, strength, power, lat. *augmentum*.

Skr. *o* = idg. *eu̯*:

skr. *bódhāmi*, I perceive, gr. *πεύθομαι* (*πυνθάνομαι*), goth. *biuda*.

ved. *joṣṭar-*, loving, cf. gr. *γευστήριον*.

Skr. *o* = idg. *ou̯*:

skr. *bubódha*, perceived, goth. *bauþ* (gr. **πεπουθα* supplanted by *πέπευθα*).

skr. *sūnó-ṣ*, of the (a) son, goth. *sunaus*.

Skr. *oḍh* sometimes goes back on idg. *eǵh* + *t* (see § 61):

skr. *vóḍhum*, to carry, cf. *váhāmi*, lat. *vehō*.

skr. *sóḍhum*, to overpower, to withstand, cf. *sáhāmi*, gr. *ἔχω*.

§ 31. **Skr. ṛ, ṝ, ḷ, ḹ.** Skr. *ṛ* corresponds to idg *r̥* as well as to idg. *l̥*. The *ṝ* in some cases of the *-ar-* (*-tar-*) stems is not yet fully explained. Skr. *ḷ* is found in a few forms and derivates of the root *kalp-*, but even here it is a prācritism (*kḷptá-s* instead of **kṛptá-s*). The *ḹ* is not met with in any word: the Hindu grammarians added it to the alphabet only for the sake of symmetry.

Skr. *ṛ* = idg. *r̥*:

skr. *ṛ́kṣa-s*, bear, gr. *ἄρκτος*, lat. *ursus.*

ved. *kṛ́p-*, appearance, shape, lat. *corpus.*

skr. *mṛtá-s*, dead, ohg. *mord.*

Skr. *ṛ* = idg. *l̥*:

skr. *pṛthú-ṣ*, wide, gr. *πλατύς.*

skr. *bhṛ́gu-ṣ* n. propr., cf. lat. *fulgur, fulgeo: flagrāre:* gr. *φλόξ, φλέγω.*

§ 32. **Skr. āi.** In skr. *āi* have fallen together the idg. tautosyllabic combinations *āi̯*, *ēi̯*, *ōi̯*.

Skr. *āi* = idg. *āi̯*:

ved. dat. sing. fem. *suvapatyā́i*, to her who has good offspring, gr. *χώρᾳ*, goth. *gibai.*

Skr. *āi* = idg. *ēi̯*:

skr. *ádāikṣam*, I showed, gr. *ἔδειξα.*

Skr. *āi* = idg. *ōi̯*: no example.

§ 33. **Skr. āu.** In skr. *āu* have fallen together the idg. tautosyllabic combinations *āu̯*, *ēu̯*, *ōu̯*.

Skr. *āu* = idg. *āu̯*:

skr. *nā́u-ṣ*, ship, gr. *ναῦς.*

Skr. *āu* = idg. *ēu̯*:

skr. *dyā́u-ṣ*, heaven, gr. *Ζεύς.*

Skr. *āu* = idg. *ōu̯*:

skr. *gā́u-ṣ*, cow, bull, gr. *βοῦς*, lat. *bōs* (**vōs*), ohg. *chuo.*

PART II.

SYSTEM OF CONSONANTS.

A. The representation of the Indogermanic consonants in Sanskrit.

§ 34. **The Indogermanic consonants in general.** The mother-language had semivowels, nasals, liquids, explosives and spirants.

Semivowels: *i̯*, *u̯*.

Nasals: *m* (labial), *n* (dental), *ṅ* (guttural), *ñ* (palatal). The *ṅ* only is met with before velars and middle gutturals (see below), the *ñ* before palatals, but *m* and *n* were found at the beginning of words, between vowels and in pausa. Further *m* occurred before labial and dental mutes, *n* before dental mutes.

Liquids: *r*, *l*. The existence of *l* in the mother-language appears not only from the fact, that the languages of Europe in general agree with each other in the distribution of *r* and *l*, but also from Fortunatov's rule (§ 44).

Explosives: To the explosives belongs the spiritis lenis, which is not indicated in writing. The other explosives were labial, dental or guttural. There were three series of gutturals, which are not determinated with perfect physiological accuracy, viz. the so-called velars (most backward in the mouth; they were formed by the hindermost part of the tongue and the soft palate), the middle gutturals (a little more in the fore-part of the mouth; perhaps their explosion took place at the hard palate), the palatals (most forward in the mouth; their explosion took place at the foremost part of the hard palate). Some scholars believe, that there were no palatal explosives in the mother-language, and assume palatal spirants instead of them (see Bechtel 370 sqq.): against this theory Museum, 1, 94 sq.

So we have to assume the following series of explosives:

Labials: *p*, *ph*, *b*, *bh*.
Dentals: *t*, *th*, *d*, *dh*.
Velars: *q*, *qh*, *g̴*, *g̴h*.
Middle gutturals: *k*, *kh*, *g*, *gh*.
Palatals: *k̂*, *k̂h*, *ĝ*, *ĝh*.

About *ph*, *th*, *qh*, *kh*, *k̂h* (tenues aspiratae) and *bh*, *dh*, *g̴h*, *gh*, *ĝh* (mediae aspiratae) is to be observed, that they are compound consonants, consisting of an explosive + *h*.

Bezzenberger (Bezz. Beitr. 16, 234 sqq.) has proved, that there was an original difference between the gutturals, which in the western group are represented by labialized gutturals (see § 52), and those, which in all dialects are preserved as pure gutturals (cf. Meillet, Mém. de la Soc. de Ling. 8, 277, sqq. and Hoffmann, Bezz. Beitr. 18, 149 sqq., who do not convince me).

As we have said above, there were also spirants in the mother-language, viz. *s*, *z*, *j*, *v*, *þ*, *đ*. The existence of the idg. *z* was discovered by Osthoff (Kuhn's Zeitschr. 23, 87 sqq.). About *þ* and *đ* see Brugmann 1, 409 and Kretschmer, Kuhn's

Zeitschr. 31, 429 sqq. Von Fierlinger (Kuhn's Zeitschr. 27, 478 sq. note) supposes, that also in those cases, where an Indian *h* corresponds to a Greek γ, a spirant may have been the original sound: this theory however is quite uncertain and would not even seem very probable. In no case we can accept Kozlovskij's theory about an idg. χ (Arch. f. slav. phil. 11, 383 sqq.): see my remarks on this subject (Arch. f. slav. phil. 16, 380 sq.).

Semivowels.

§ 35. **Idg. i̯.** The idg. *i̯* remained unchanged in Indian, except in the tautosyllabic combinations *ai̯*, *ei̯*, *oi̯*, which in Aryan fell together in *ai̯* and in Indian were contracted to *e* (see § 7, 9, 11):

idg. **i̯ó-s*: skr. *yá-s*, who, gr. ὅς.

idg. **i̯ḗqr̥-t*, genit. **i̯eqnós*: skr. *yákr̥t* (with *a* instead of *ā* by the influence of the casus obliqui, cf. avest. *yākarĕ*), liver, gr. ἧπαρ, lat. *jecur*.

idg. **i̯ag̑nó-s*: skr. *yajñá-s*, sacrifice, gr. ἁγνός.

idg. **i̯udh-*: skr. *yúdh-*, battle, gr. ὑσμίνη.

idg. **i̯usm-*: skr. *yuṣma-*, you, gr. ὑμεῖς, lesb. ὔμμες, cf. goth. *jūs*.

idg. **ēi̯m̥(m)*: skr. *áyam*, I went, gr. ᾖα (*ἦα).

idg. **tréi̯es*: skr. *tráyas*, three, gr. τρεῖς, lat. *trēs*, goth. *þreis* (from **þrii̯iz*).

idg. **médhi̯o-s*: skr. *mádhya-s*, gr. μέσσος, μέσος, lat *medius*, goth. *midjis*.

idg. **g̑i̯ā́*, **g̑ii̯ā́*: skr. *jyā́*, bowstring, lith. *gija*, thread, cf. gr. βιός, bow.

In Vedic there was an exchange of *y* and *iy* after consonants, which doubtlessly goes back to the Indogermanic period (see Brugmann 1, 112 sq. 115 sq.).

Before *ĭ* at the beginning of words *i̯* seems to have disappeared (cf. § 36).

§ 36. **Idg. u̯.** The idg. *u̯* remained unchanged in Indian, except in the tautosyllabic combinations *au̯*, *eu̯*, *ou̯*, which in Aryan fell together in *au̯* and in Indian were contracted to *o* (see § 7, 9, 11):

idg. **u̯éqos*, **u̯éqes-*: skr. *vácas*, word, gr. ἔπος.

idg. **u̯ōq-s*, genit. **u̯oqós*: skr. *vā́k*, voice, lat. *vōx*, gr. ὀπ-.

idg. **u̯ói̯da*: skr. *véda*, I know, gr. οἶδα, goth. *wait*.

idg. **u̯ói̯k̂o-s*: skr. *veça-s*, house, gr. οἶκος, cf. lat. *vīcus*, goth. *weihs* and skr. *víç-*, people.

idg. **néu̯o-s*: skr. *náva-s*, new, gr. νέος, lat. *novus*, cf. ved. *návya-s*, gr. νεῖος, lat. *Novius*, goth. *niujis*.

idg. **bhāĝheu̯es*: skr. *bāhávas*, arms (plur. of *bāhú-ṣ*), gr. πήχεες, πήχεις.

idg. **k̂u̯es-*: skr. *çvásimi*, I breathe, I sigh, lat. *queror*.

idg. **su̯ādú-s*: skr. *svādú-ṣ*, sweet, gr. ἡδύς, lat. *suāvis* (after the femin. idg. **su̯ādu̯í*, cf. lat. *tenuis*: skr. *tanú-ṣ*), ags. *swéte*, os. *swōti*.

idg. **sólu̯o-s*: skr. *sárva-s*, entire, all, gr. ὅλος, οὖλος.

In Vedic there was an exchange of *v* and *uv* after consonants, which doubtlessly goes back to the Indogermanic period (see Brugmann, 1, 140, 143).

Before *ŭ* (idg. *ŭ*, *ə*) at the beginning of words *u̯* was lost in Indian: examples of this rule (*úraṇa-s*, *ūrdhvá-s*, *ūrmí-ṣ*, *ū́rṇā*) are mentioned in § 13. Osthoff (Morphol. unters. 4, X sq. note) assumes an analogous loss of *i̯* before *ĭ* (perf. *iyā́ja*, desiderat. *íyakṣ-*: *yájati*, worships; intens. *iyasyate*: *yásyati*, gets tired with working).

In some Indian dialects *v* seems to have been changed to *m*. Traces of this change are perhaps ved. *áma-s*, this: avest. *ava-*, oslav. *ovŭ* and skr. *çyāmá-s*, dark: *çyāvá-s*, oslav. *sivŭ*. But it can be hardly doubted, that sometimes there were forms with *m* by the side of the original with *u̯* in the mother-language. About the suffixes with *u̯*, resp. *m* see Brugmann 2, 189, 379 &c.: most striking is ved. *dámane*, gr. δόμεναι: ved. *dāváne*, gr. δοϝέναι. Cf. also skr. *drámāmi*, I run, gr. ἔδραμον, δέδρομα, δρόμος: skr. *drávāmi*.

Nasals.

§ 37. **Idg. m.** In general the idg. *m* remained unchanged. Perhaps we may assume, that *mr* at the beginning of words became *br* in Indian (skr. *brávīti*, speaks: avest. *mraoiti*, see Osthoff, Morphol. Unters. 5, 130 sqq., but with *mr* skr. *mriyáte*: lat. *morior* and other words).

Instances of idg. *m* = skr. *m*:

idg. **mātḗ(r)*: skr. *mātā́*, mother, gr. μήτηρ, lat. *māter*, ohg. *muoter*.

idg. **m̥tó-s*: skr. *matá-s*, thought, gr. -ματος, lat. *-mentus*, goth. *munds*.

idg. **mr̥tí-s*: skr. *mr̥ti-ṣ*, death, lat. *mors*, genit. *mortis*.

idg. **mnā-*: skr. *mnāta-s*, mentioned, gr. μιμνήσκω, μνήσω, μέμνημαι.

idg. **mlā-*: skr. *mlā́yāmi*, I wither, gr. βλᾱ́ξ, genit. βλᾱκός, slack, lazy, stupid (**mlā-k-s*).

idg. **u̯em-*: skr. *vámāmi*, *vámimi*, I vomit, gr. ἐμέω, lat. *vomō*.

idg. **smei̯-*: skr. *smáyate*, smiles, gr. φιλομμειδής, μειδιάω, lat. *mīrus* (skr. *vi-smayate*, is astonished), engl. *smile*.

idg. **g̑hormó-s*: skr. *gharmá-s*, warm, warmth, heat, lat. *formus*, goth. *warms*, cf. gr. θερμός.

idg. **au̯gmen-*: ved. *ojmán-*, strength, power, lat. *augmen*, *augmentum*.

idg. **ĝómbho-s*: ved. *jámbha-s*, set of teeth, tooth, gr. γόμφος, ohg. *chamb*, engl. *comb*.

idg. **tó-m*: skr. *tám*, gr. τόν, lat. *is-tum*, goth. *þan-a*, acc. pron. dem. **to-*.

idg. **bhérontōm*: skr. 3 pers. plur. imperat. med. *bhárantām*, they must bear, gr. 3 pers. plur. imperat. act. φερόντων.

Before *t* and *u̯* the idg. *m* became *n*:

idg. **g̑émtu*: ved. *gántu*, he must go.

idg. **g̑eg̑m̥mu̯ós*: ved. *jaganván*, having gone (cf. § 18).

The idg. combination *ms* is represented by *n* at the end of words, by *ṁs* between vowels:

idg. **dems*: ved. *dán*, of the house, gr. δες- in δεσπότης (ved. *pátir dán*, *dámpati-ṣ*).

idg. **ómso-s*: skr. *áṁsa-s*, shoulder, goth. *ams*, cf. gr. ὦμος and lat. *umerus*.

§ 38 **Idg. n.** In general the idg. *n* remained unchanged:

idg. **nắu̯-s*: skr. *náu-ṣ*, ship, gr. ναῦς, cf. lat. *nāvis* and icel. *nó-* (see Streitberg, Zur germanischen sprachgeschichte, Strassburg 1892, 49 sqq.).

idg. **nébhos*: skr. *nábhas*, sky, gr. νέφος, cf. gr. νεφέλη, lat. *nebula*, ohg. *nebul*.

idg. **nōmn̥*: skr. *nắma* (*n*), lat. *nōmen*, cf. gr. ὄνομα and goth. *namō*.

idg. **séno-s*: ved. *sána-s*, old, gr. fem. ἕνη, cf. lat. *senex* and goth. *sineigs*.

idg. **u̯idmenai̯*: ved. *vidmáne*, to know, gr. ἴδμεναι.

idg. **su̯épno-s*, **supnó-s*: skr. *svápna-s*, sleep, lat. *somnus*, icel. *svefn*, with idg. *u* gr. ὕπνος.

idg. **bhéndhono-m*: skr. *bándhana-m* binding, band, bond,

goth. *bindan*, cf. skr. *bándhu-ṣ*, connection, relative, friend, gr. πενθερός, father in law, and lat. *offendix*, *offendimentum*.

idg. **tékþon*: skr. voc. *tákṣan*, carpenter, gr. τέκτον.

After *c* and *j* (idg. *q*, *k*, resp. *g*, *g*, *ĝ*) *n* was palatalized: so idg. **i̯aĝnó-s* became skr. *yajñá-s*, sacrifice. The only instance of *ñ* (idg. *n*) after *c* is skr. *yācñā́*, request: *yā́cate*, asks.

After *ṣ*, *r*, *ṛ*, *ṝ* the dental nasal was turned into the lingual *ṇ*: idg. **kr̥sno-s* (**qr̥sno-s?*): skr. *kr̥ṣṇá-s*, black, opruss. *kirsna-*, cf. oslav. *črĭnŭ*.

idg. **usnó-s*: skr. *uṣṇá-s*, hot: *óṣāmi*, I burn, gr. εὕω, lat. *ūrō*. Cf. lith. *usnis*, thistle.

idg. **érnos*: ved. *árṇas*, flood, stream, cf. ohg. *ernust*, ags. *eornost* (see my Etym. wb. der got. sprache s. v. *arniba*).

idg. **mr̥nā́mi*: ved. *mr̥ṇā́mi*, I crush, gr. med. μάρναμαι.

idg. **tr̥no-m*: skr. *tŕ̥ṇa-m*, grass, cf. goth. *þaúrnus*.

Not only if *ṣ*, *r*, *ṛ*, *ṝ* immediately preceded, the dental *n* was lingualized: the change of *n* to *ṇ* took place, at whatever distance from it the lingual consonant or vowel might be found, unless there intervened a palatal affricate, a *ç*, a dental or a lingual (see Whitney § 189 sqq.). Instances:

skr. *dvéṣāṇi*, 1 pers. sing. praes. conj. (imperat.) of *dvéṣmi*, I hate.

ved. *cákṣaṇa-m*, sight, appearance: *cáṣṭe*, appears, sees, looks.

skr. *Rudréṇa*, instr. sing. of *Rudrá-s*.

skr. *vā́riṇe*, dat. sing. of *vā́ri*, water.

skr. *krīṇā́mi*, I buy, cf. gr. ἐπριάμην.

skr. *cíkīrṣamāṇa-s*, part. praes. of *cíkīrṣate*, desires to do (desid. of *karóti*, does).

The idg. combination *ns* is represented by *n* at the end of words (cf. Lorentz, Bezz. Beitr. 21, 173 sqq.), by *ṁs* between vowels:

idg. **u̯l̥qons*: skr. acc. plur. *vṛ́kān*, wolves, cf. gr. λύκους, lat. *equōs*, *lupōs*, goth. *wulfans*, *dagans* (also skr. acc. plur. *agnī́n*, *paraçū́n*, cf. goth. *anstins*, *sununs* &c.).

idg. **ĝhans-*: skr. *haṁsá-s*, goose, swan, gr. χήν, ohg. *gans*, cf. lat. *anser*.

About idg. *ln* (*rn*), skr. *ṇ* see § 44.

§ 39. **Idg. ṅ.** The idg. *ṅ* remained unchanged, unless the following guttural (resp. velar) was palatalized by the influence of a palatal vowel:

idg. **oṅko-s*: skr. *aṅká-s*, lap, hook, gr. ὄγκος, lat. *uncus*, cf. goth. *hals-agga*.

idg. **bhoṅgo-s*, **bhoṅgā*: skr. *bhaṅgá-s*, wave, lith. *banga*.

But *ṅ* became *ñ*, if the following guttural (resp. velar) was changed into a palatal affricate:

idg. **péṅqe*: skr. *páñca*, five, gr. πέντε, lat. *quinque*, goth. *fimf*.

§ 40. **Idg. ñ.** The idg. *ñ* remained unchanged before idg. *ĝ*, skr. *j*, but it became *ṁ* before idg. *k̂*, skr. *ç* and before idg. *ĝh*, skr. *h*. In other words: if the following palatal guttural became a spirant, *ñ* was reduced to anusvāra.

idg. **ēnóñk̂a*: skr. *ānáṁça*, I attained (perf. of *açnómi*, idg. **n̥k̂néu̯mi*), cf. *áṁça-*, portion, part, gr. ἤνεγκον, ἐνήνοχα, lat. *nanciscor*.

idg. **áñĝhos*: ved. *áṁhas*, distress, lat. *angus-* in *angustus*, cf. gr. ἄγχω, lat. *angō* &c.

Liquids.

§ 41. **The liquids in general.** Nowadays no one doubts any more, but that the mother-language, possessed at least two liquids, viz. *r* and *l*. Since the clever article of Fortunatov on the representation of dental + liquid in Indian, it may be called very probable, that the ancient difference between *r* and *l* still existed in the Aryan period. In Iranian *r* and *l* fell together into *r* and in the Vedic dialect of Indian *l* is but rare: in most cases epic and class. *l* is represented by ved. *r*. Therefore we need not be surprised, that the older linguists considered *l* as younger than *r*.

Yet it can not be denied, that in as early a period as the Indogermanic there often stood forms with *r* and *l* side by side with each other (*l*:*r* in suffixes see Brugmann 2, § 62, 74—77, 98, 107, 119—122; in root-syllables Persson, Studien zur lehre v. d. wurzelerweiterung &c., Upsala 1891, 59—67, cf. P. B. Beitr. 17, 437 sqq. and my Etym. wb. der got. sprache s. v. *alhs*, *baírhts*, *biraubōn*, *gras*, *grēdus*, *hrūk*, *kalbō*, *stilan*). This Indogermanic change of *r* and *l* does not properly belong to the province of Indian phonetics and so we may leave it unnoticed. Likewise such cases as skr. *bhunákti*: goth. *brūkjan*, skr. *bhanákti*: goth. *brikan* are to be explained by phonetic rules of the mother-language.

§ 42. **Idg. r.** In general the idg. *r* remained unchanged. Instances are:

idg. **régi̯ō*: skr. *rájyāmi*, I am (get) red, affected with a strong feeling, gr. *ῥέζω*.

idg. **rē-s*: skr. *rā́-s*, wealth, lat. *rēs*.

idg. **rēk̂-s*, stem **rēĝ-*: skr. *rā́ṭ* (instead of **rāk* from **rākṣ*, which was to be expected), lat. *rēx*.

idg. **reu̯d-*: skr. *ródimi*, I weep, lat. *rūdō*, ags. *réotan*.

idg. **bhérō*: skr. *bhárāmi*, I bear, gr. *φέρω*, lat. *ferō*, goth. *baíra*.

idg. **péri*: skr. *pári*, around, gr. *πέρι*, lat. *per*, goth. *faír-*.

idg. **smérō*: skr. *smárāmi*, I remember, cf. lat. *memor*.

idg. **dedórk̂a*: skr. *dadárça*, I saw, gr. δέδορκα.

idg. **ger-*: skr. *jāgármi*, I wake, gr. ἐγείρω, ἐγρήγορα.

idg. **grasó*: skr. *grásāmi*, I eat, I devour, gr. γράω.

idg. **qrīnámi*: skr. *krīṇámi*, I buy, cf. gr. ἐπριάμην.

idg. **máter*: skr. vocat. *mátar*, mother, gr. μῆτερ.

About the combinations of *r* with dentals see § 44. Unexplained is the *l* in cases as skr. *luñcāmi*, I pull out, I pull off, I husk: gr. ὀρύσσω, lat. *runcāre*; skr. *lumpámi*, I break (already ved., by the side of *rúpyāmi*, I have belly-ache): lat. *rumpō*, ags. *réofan*, and many others. In some of them we must assume an Indogermanic change of *r* and *l*.

§ 43. **Idg. l.** In Vedic the idg. *l* has fallen together with *r*, except when followed by a dental. The words, containing *l* are to be considered as loans from an other dialect. In the epic and classical language the original *l* is represented in some cases by *l*, in other cases by *r*; often the same word occurs in two forms, with *l* and with *r*. The distribution of the two liquids in the Brāhmaṇa's is nearly the same as in classical Sanskrit. I am inclined to believe, that the idg. *l* regularly remained unchanged in Sanskrit: the forms with *r* may have been borrowed from other dialects. Hence it appears, that the Sanskrit of Madhyadeça is not a younger form of the western dialect, in which the hymns of the Ṛgveda have come down to us.

Idg. *l* = skr. *l*:

idg. **lambetai̯*: skr. *lámbate*, hangs down (already Çat. Br., but Rgv. *rámbate*), cf. lat. *lābor*.

idg. **léiĝhmi*: skr. *léhmi*, I lick (but ved. *réhmi*), cf. gr. λείχω, lat. *lingō* and goth. *-laigōn*.

idg. **limpó*: skr. *limpámi*, I smear (already Athv. and Brāhm., but Rgv. *rip* — except however I, 191, 1-4 *alipsata*), cf.

gr. λίπος, λιπαρός, ἀλείφω, ἀλοιφή, lat. *lippus*, goth. *bi-leiban*, *laiba*, *liban*.

idg. **lubh-*, **leu̯bh-*: skr. *lúbhyāmi*, I desire (already Athv. and Brāhm., even Rgv. 10, 103, 12 *lobháyantī*), lat. *lubet*, goth. *liufs*.

idg. **təlā́*: skr. *tulā́*, balance (already Vājasaneyi-saṁhitā and Brāhm.; with unexplained *u* instead of *i*), cf. gr. τάλαντον, τελαμών, lat. *tollō*, goth. *þulan*.

idg. **alpo-s* (**olpo-s*?): skr. *álpa-s*, small, cf. lith. *alpti*, to languish, to swoon away, *alpnas*, weak, fainted (also gr. ἀλαπαδνός?).

Idg. *l* = skr. *r*:

idg. **léksō*, **əléksō*: skr. *rákṣāmi*, I guard, I protect, gr. ἀλέξω.

idg. **lelói̯qa*: skr. *riréca*, I left, gr. λέλοιπα, goth. *laihw*, perf. of skr. *riṇácmi*, gr. λείπω, goth. *leihwa*.

idg. **léu̯dhō*: skr. *róhāmi* (ved. also *ródhāmi*, which is the older form), I rise, I grow, goth. *liuda*, cf. gr. ἐλεύσομαι, εἰλήλουθα.

idg. **pel-*, **plē-*: skr. *píparmi*, I fill, gr. πίμπλημι, πλήρης, lat. *im-pleō*, *plēnus*, cf. with *l̥* goth. *fulls*.

idg. **pléthetai̯*: skr. *práthate*, broadens, cf. *pṛthú-ṣ*, broad, gr. πλατύς.

About the combinations of *l* with dentals see § 44.

§ 44. **Combinations of r and l with dentals.** Fortunatov (Bezz. Beitr. 6, 215 sqq.) has given the following rule: *r* + dental remained unchanged, but in the combinations of *l* and a following dental the *l* disappeared and the dental was lingualized. It is to be noticed, that the word *dental* is taken here in its widest sense. Bechtel 382 sqq., Windisch (Kuhn's Zeitschr. 27, 168), Darbishire (Relliquiae philologicae, Cambridge 1895, 202 sqq. 241 sqq.) and many other scholars have accepted this rule, but Brugmann 1, 213, Bartholomae (Idg. forschungen 3, 157 sqq.), J. Schmidt (Kritik der sonantentheorie 1 sq. note) and Wackernagel 1, 171 prefer to believe, that all those linguals, which go back on a combination of liquid + dental are due to Prācritic influence.

Examples of *r* + dental:

idg. **kértō*: skr. *kártāmi* (epic, the classical praesens is *kṛntā́mi*), I cut, lith. *kertu*.

idg. **u̯értō*: skr. *vártāmi* (more common med. *várte*), I turn, move, go on, abide, exist, am, am present, lat. *vertō*, goth. *waírþa*.

idg. **mérdō*: skr. *márdāmi*, I press, squeeze, crush, destroy, cf. lat. *mordeō* (= skr. causat. *mardáyāmi*).

idg. **pérdetai̯*: skr. *párdate* (Dhātup.), breaks wind, gr. *πέρδεται*, cf. hg. *firzen*, *furzen*.

idg. **ardho-s* (**ordho-s*?): skr. *ardhá-s*, half, cf. lith. *ardyti*, to separate.

idg. **ghordho-s*: skr. *gardha-s*, desire, avidity, cf. goth. *grēdus*, hunger.

idg. **kórno-s*: skr. *kárṇa-s*, ear.

idg. **u̯órno-s*: skr. *várṇa-s*, cover, outside, color, caste, sound, akin to *vṛṇómi*, I cover, *várūtha-m*, cover, protection, gr. *ἔρυσθαι*, goth. *warjan* &c.

idg. **dhérsō*: skr. *dhárṣāmi* (more common *dhṛṣṇómi*), I dare, cf. gr. *θαρσέω*, *θαρρέω*, *θαρσαλεός*, *θρασύς* &c., goth. *ga-dars*.

idg. **u̯ersā*: skr. *varṣā́*, rain, gr. *ἔρση*, *ἕρση*, *ἐέρση*.

Examples of *l* + dental:

idg. **palto-s*: skr. *paṭa-s*, woven stuff, cloth, garment, cf. oslav. *platĭno*, russ. *polotnó*, linen, perhaps also skr. *paṭála-m*, cover, veil, mass, gr. (thrac.?) *πέλτη*, a little shield, and icel. *feldr*, cover.

idg. **paltu-s*: skr. *paṭu-ṣ*, sharp, cf. gr. *πλατύς*, saltish, brack.

idg. **sphalt-*: skr. *sphá̄ṭāmi*, I burst (Dhātup. *visaraṇe*), ohg. *spaltan* (from *spaldan* with germ. *d* from *þ* by Verner's law).

idg. **u̯alto-s*: skr. *vaṭa-s* (*vaṭa-m*, *vaṭī*), snare, cf. lith. *valtis*, thread, net, russ. *vólotĭ*, thread.

idg. **ĝhŏ̆lto-*: skr. *hāṭaka-m*, gold (also „Goldland", a certain country in India, the inhabitants of which were called *Hāṭakās*), oslav. *zlato*, russ. *zóloto*, cf. with *l̥* goth. *gulþ*.

idg. **gelth-* (**ĝelth-*?): skr. *jaṭhára-m*, belly, womb, goth. *kilþei* (cf. with *r* skr. *jartú-*, vulva, Uṇādisūtra).

idg. **kulth-*: skr. *kuṭhāra-*, axe, lat. *culter*.

idg. **kəlno-s*: skr. *kiṇa-s*, callosity, lat. *callus* (*callum*).

idg. **kulni-s*, **kulno-s*: skr. *kuṇi-ṣ*, lame of one arm, gr. *κυλλός*.

idg. **ŏ̆lní-s*: skr. *āṇí-ṣ* (*aṇi-ṣ*), the leg immediately above the knee, linch-pin, cf. gr. *ὠλένη*, lat. *ulna*, goth. *aleina* and ohg. *lun*, os. *lunisa*, ags. *lynes*, linch-pin (with *lu* from *l̥*?).

idg. **pălní-s*: skr. *pāṇí-ṣ*, hand, cf. gr. *παλάμη*, lat. *palma* and ags. *folm*.

idg. **pélno-s*: skr. *paṇa-s*, wager, stake, prize, wages, a coin &c., lith. *pelnas*, wages, oslav. *plěnŭ*, booty, cf. gr. *πωλέω* and ohg. *fāli*.

idg. **u̯ălnī*: ved. *vá̄ṇī*, reed, rush, cf. goth. *walus*.

idg. **bhăls-*: skr. *bhá̄ṣate*, speaks, *bhá̄ṣati*, barks, lith. *balsas*, voice, tone, icel. *bjalla*, engl. *bell*.

idg. **lals-*: skr. *lá̄ṣāmi*, I desire, cf. *lālasa-s*, desirous, gr. *λιλαίομαι* and goth. *lustus* (*lu* from *l̥*?).

idg. **pěls-*: skr. *pāṣāṇá-s*, ved. *pāṣyà-*, stone, gr. *πέλλα· λίθος*, cf. ohg. *felis*.

The apparent exceptions to Fortunatov's rule may be explained as prācritisms. Such cases are:

skr. *bhaṭa-s*, soldier: *bhṛtá-s*, hired (cf. gr. *φέρω*).

skr. *káṭa-s*, mat: *kartana-m*, spinning (cf. gr. *κύρτος*).

skr. *kaṭú-ṣ*, sharp: **kartú-ṣ* (cf. lith. *kartus*).

skr. *naṭa-s*, dancer, actor: *nartaka-s*, dancer (*nṛ́tyāmi*, I dance).

By no means all linguals go back on *l* (*r*) + dental, but they are often original dentals, which are lingualized by Prācritic influence. Instances are skr. *aṭāmi*, I roam, I wander about: ved. *átāmi*; skr. *bhaṇāmi*, I speak: ved. *bhánāmi* &c.

§ 45. **Metathesis of r.** On this subject see Brugmann 1, 214 and Persson, Studien zur lehre v. d. wurzelerweiterung 218 sqq. Instances of *ra* : *ar*: fut. *drakṣyámi*, perf. 2 pers. sing. *dadrásṭha*, inf. *drásṭum* from the root *darç-*, idg. **derk̂-*, to see; perf. 2 pers. sing. *tatráptha* (*tatárptha*) from the root *tarp-*, idg. **terp-*, to be satisfied; fut. *srapsyámi* (*sarpsyámi*), aor. *ásrāpsam* (*ásārpsam*) from the root *sarp-*, idg. **serp-*, to creep.

Labial explosives.

§ 46. **Idg. p.** Idg. *p* = skr. *p*:

idg. **pətḗ(r)*: skr. *pitá*, gr. *πατήρ*, lat. *pater*, goth. *fadar*.

idg. **pərós*: skr. *purás*, in front, forward, before, gr. *πάρος*, cf. goth. *faúra*.

idg. **pelek̂u-s*: skr. *paraçú-ṣ*, axe, gr. *πέλεκυς*, cf. goth. *filhan*, *filigri*.

idg. **pṛk̂ni-s*: skr. *pṛ́çni-ṣ*, speckled, cf. gr. *περκνός* and perhaps ohg. *forhana*, trout.

idg. **perut*: skr. *parut*, last year, cf. gr. *πέρυσι*, dor. *πέρυτι*, mhg. *vert*.

idg. **pró*: skr. *prá-*, forward, onward, gr. πρό, goth. *fra-*, cf. lat. *prōd*, *prō*.

idg. **pléu̯ō*: skr. *plávāmi*, I float, I swim &c., gr. πλέω, cf. lat. *pluit* and with suffix *-d* ags. *fléotan*.

idg. **népōt-s*: ved. *nápāt*, descendant, grandson, lat. *nepōs*, ohg. *nefo*.

idg. **su̯épno-s*: skr. *svápna-s*, sleep, dream, lat. *somnus*, icel. *svefn*, cf. gr. ὕπνος.

idg. **sérpō*: skr. *sárpāmi*, I creep &c., gr. ἕρπω, lat. *serpō*.

idg. **spéḱ-s*: ved. *spáṭ* (instead of **spak*, stem *spaç-*), lat. *-spex* in *auspex*, *haruspex*, cf. skr. *páçyāmi* (Dhātup. also *spáçāmi*), lat. *specio*, ohg. *spehōn*.

How far the Aryan *ph* (skr. *ph*, iran. *f*) goes back on idg. *ph*, is still unsettled (cf. Hoffmann, Bezz. Beitr. 18, 154 sqq.). Instances of skr. *ph*, iran. *f*:

skr. *kapha-*, phlegm, avest. *kafa-*.

skr. *çaphá-*, hoof, avest. *safa-*.

§ 47. **Idg. b.** Idg. *b* = skr. *b* (cf. P. B. Beitr. 18, 236 sqq. 20, 325 sqq.):

idg. **bolo-m*: skr. *bála-m*, strength, power, cf. oslav. *bolij*, greater, larger, lat. *dē-bilis*, powerless, weak (cf. von Grienberger, Zeitschr. für deutsche philologie 27, 453 sqq. and Osthoff, Idg. forschungen 6, 1 sqq.).

idg. **bālo-s* (*ā* or *ō*?): skr. *bālá-s*, young, foolish, whiteruss. *bal*, liar, cf. also russ. *balovátĭ*, to dally, to fondle, to spoil.

idg. **balbal-*, **barbar-*: skr. *balbalā-karomi*, I stammer, *barbará-s*, stammering, gr. βάρβαρος, cf. lat. *balbus* with broken reduplication.

idg. **bal-*: ved. *balbalīti*, whirls (*Uccāir dhūmaḥ paramayā jūtyā balbalīti*, Çat. Br.), cf. gr. βαλλίζω.

idg. **buk-*: skr. *buk-kāra-s*, roar, bellow, gr. *βύκτης*, *βυκάνη*, lat. *būcina*.

idg. **belk-*, **blek-*: skr. *bárkara-s*, kid, slov. *blekati*, to bleat, *blekaš*, bleating buck.

idg. **buli-s*: skr. *buli-ṣ*, cunnus, buttock, lith. *bulìs*, buttock, cf. lat. *bulla*, bubble, lith. *bumbulas*, knob, knot, *bumbulys*, turnip, russ. *búlka*, roll (bread), dutch *peul*, husk, pulse, *puilen*, to swell (in speaking of eyes: to start from the head).

idg. **bāl-* (with *ā* or *ō*?): skr. *jam-bāla-s*, pool, mud (*jam-*, earth, + *-bāla-s*), ags. *pól*, swed. *pöl*, cf. lith. *bala* and oslav. *blato*, russ. *bolóto*.

idg. **pibō*: skr. *píbāmi*, I drink, lat. *bibō* (irish *ebaim* proves, that the first consonant was an idg. *p*).

idg. **lamb-*, **lāb-*: skr. *lámbate*, hangs down, lat. *lābitur*, cf. goth. *slēpan*, ags. *slǽpan*, to sleep, ohg. *slaf*, dutch *slap*, slack, oslav. *slabŭ*, weak.

idg. **-bd-*: ved. *upa-bdá-s*, stamping, trampling, gr. *ἐπίβδαι*, the day after a feast, cf. *πεδά*, immediately after, and skr. *pát*, foot, gr. *πούς* &c.

§ 48. **Idg. bh.** Idg. *bh* = skr. *bh*:

idg. **bhérō*: skr. *bhárāmi* (*bíbharmi*), I bear, gr. *φέρω*, lat. *ferō*, goth. *baíra*.

idg. **bhéu̯ō*: skr. *bhávāmi*, I am, cf. gr. *φύω*, lat. *fui*, ohg. *būan*.

idg. **bhrātē(r)*: skr. *bhrātā*, gr. *φρᾱτηρ*, lat. *frāter* &c.

idg. **bhrū-s*, **əbhrū-s*: skr. *bhrū-ṣ*, eye-brow, gr. *ὀφρῦς* (from **ἀφρῦς*, cf. Schmidt, Kuhn's Zeitschr. 32, 376 sqq.), cf. oslav. *brŭvĭ*, *obrŭvĭ* and ohg. *brāwa*.

idg. **nébhos*: skr. *nábhas*, cloud, sky, gr. *νέφος*, cf. gr. *νεφέλη*, lat. *nebula*, ohg. *nebul*.

idg. **ĝómbho-s*: skr. *jámbha-s*, set of teeth, tooth, gr. *γόμφος*, ohg. *chamb*.

When followed by an aspirate, *bh* lost its aspiration: idg. **bhéu̯dhō*: skr. *bódhāmi*, I perceive, goth. *biuda*, cf. gr. πυνθάνομαι, πεύθομαι.

idg. **bhn̥dhnámi*: skr. *badhnámi*, I bind, cf. *bándhana-m*, binding, band, bond, goth. *bindan*: to this root belong also skr. *bándhu-ṣ*, connection, relative, friend, gr. πενθερός and lat. *offendimentum*, *offendix*.

Idg. *bh* + *t* is represented by *bdh*: see § 49.

We must assume with von Bradke (Zeitschr. der D. Morgenl. Ges. 40, 657 sqq.), that the not very numerous cases, in which the idg. *bh* is represented by skr. *h*, are loans from a Prācritic dialect. So we find skr. *gr̥hṇámi*: ved. *gr̥bhṇámi*, I seize; skr. *hárāmi*, I bear, I take: *bhárāmi*, I bear. Cf. prākr. *pahu-*: skr. *prabhú-*, lord; prākr. *hodi*, *hoï*: skr. *bhávati*, is, &c.

Dental explosives.

§ 49. **Idg. t.** Idg. *t* = skr. *t*:

idg. **tn̥néu̯mi*: skr. *tanómi*, I stretch, cf. gr. τείνω, lat. *tendō*, *tentus*, goth. *-þanjan*. To the same root skr. *tanú-ṣ*, thin, gr. τανυ-, lat. *tenuis*, ohg. *dunni*.

idg. **tudō*: skr. *tudámi*, I push, I strike, cf. ved. *tundate*, *tundāná-*, lat. *tundō* and goth. *stautan*.

idg. **tréi̯es*: skr. *tráyas*, three, gr. τρεῖς, lat. *trēs*, goth. *þreis*.

idg. **pétō*: skr. *pátāmi*, I fly, I fall, lat. *petō*, cf. gr. πέτομαι, πίπτω.

idg. **u̯értetai̯*: skr. *vártate*, turns, rolls, goes, abides, cf. lat. *vertō*, goth. *waírþa*.

Idg. *tn* remained unchanged in Indian:

idg. **pótnī*: skr. *pátnī*, lady, mistress, wife, cf. gr. πότνια.

idg. **rətnó-m* (**retno-m*?): skr. *rátna-m* (by the side of *ratná-m*), riches, treasure (ved.), jewel, pearl, cf. § 13.

After *ṣ* the dental *t* was lingualized:

idg. **oḱtṓ(u̯)*: skr. *aṣṭā́* (ved.), *aṣṭā́u*, eight, gr. *ὀκτώ*, lat. *octō*, goth. *ahtau*.

idg. **ustó-s*: skr. *uṣṭá-s*, burned, lat. *ustus*.

Before *c* the dental *t* was palatalized:

idg. **utko-*, **utke-*: skr. *ucca-* (from **utca-*), high, derived from idg. **ŭd*, skr. *úd*, up, forth, out, goth. *ūt*, ags. *út*.

Akin to the assimilation of *tc* to *cc* was the transition of *tç* to *cch*: so *pacchás*, in hemistichs, goes back on **pat-çás*, **pad-çás*, derived from *pad-*, *pād-*, foot, quarter of a stanza.

The idg. combination *lt* became *ṭ*, see § 44.

Very difficult are the combinations of mediae aspiratae with *t*, which seem to be changed to mediae + *dh* before the end of the Indogermanic period.

Idg. *bh* + *t* = skr. *bdh*:

ved. *dabdhá-s*, harmed, hurted, deceived: *dabhnómi*.

skr. *labdhá-s*, seized, taken, got: *lábhe*.

Idg. *dh* + *t* = skr. *ddh*:

skr. *baddhá-s*, bound: *badhnā́mi*.

skr. *buddhá-s*, perceived, awake: *bódhāmi*.

Idg. *g̑h* + *t* and *gh* + *t* = skr. *gdh*:

skr. *dagdhá-s*, burned: *dáhāmi*.

Idg. *ĝh* + *t* = skr. *ḍh*:

ved. *sāḍhá-s*, conquered: *sáhāmi*.

skr. *ūḍhá-s*, carried: *váhāmi*.

How far the Aryan *th* (skr. *th*, iran. *þ*) represents an idg. *th*, is not sufficiently clear. A certain case of idg. *th* is the suffix of the 2 pers. sing. perf. *-tha*:

idg. **u̯óittha*: skr. *véttha*, thou knowest, gr. *οἶσθα*, cf. goth. *waist* and see Zubatý, Kuhn's Zeitschr. 31, 4.

Instances of skr. *th*, iran. *þ*:

skr. *rátha-*, chariot, avest. *raþa-*.

skr. *pṛthú-*, wide, avest. *pĕrĕþu-*.

§ 50. **Idg. d.** Idg. *d* = skr. *d*:

idg. **didōmi*: skr. *dádāmi*, I give (**didāmi*), gr. δίδωμι, cf. lat. *dō*.

idg. **déḱm̥*: skr. *dáça*, ten, gr. δέκα, lat. *decem*, goth. *taíhun*.

idg. **dru-*: ved. *dru-*, wood, gr. δρυτόμος, δρῦς, cf. goth. *triu* (idg. **dreu̯-*), gr. δόρυ (idg. **dóru*), skr. *dā́ru* (idg. **dōru*).

idg. **du̯ō(u̯)*: ved. *dvā́*, skr. *dvā́u*, two, gr. δύω, lat. *duō*, cf. goth. *twai*.

idg. **sédos*: skr. *sádas*, seat, gr. ἕδος: skr. root *sad-*, to sit, lat. *sedeō*, goth. *sitan* &c.

idg. **skhind-*: skr. *chindánti*, they cut off, gr. σχινδαλμός, splinter, lat. *scindō* (cf. goth. *skaidan*, idg. root **skhai̯t-*).

During or more likely long before the Aryan period *dd*, *ddh* were changed to *zd*, *zdh*. In Iranian the *z* of these combinations was preserved, but in Indian it disappeared after having developed an *i*. Example:

idg. **deddhí* (or already **dezdhí*): ar. **dazdhi*, avest. *dazdi*, skr. *dehí* (instead of **dedhí* from **daidhí*, **daizdhí*), give.

In certain cases *zd* became *žd* in Aryan, from which skr. *ḍ* (see § 63):

idg. **nizdó-s*: skr. *nīḍá-s*, nest, lat. *nīdus*, ohg. *nest*.

About the lingualization of *d* in *ld* see § 44.

Idg. *dn* was assimilated in Indian to *nn* (cf. however Bartholomae, Studien zur idg. sprachgeschichte 2, Halle 1891, 94 sqq.):

idg. **édno-m*: skr. *ánna-m*, food, rice, cf. gr. ἐδανός from **edənó-s*.

idg. **bhidnó-s*: skr. *bhinná-s*, split: *bhinádmi*, I split.

idg. **tudnó-s*: skr. *tunná-s*, pushed: *tudā́mi*, I push.

Finally it should be mentioned, that skr. *dj* became *jj*. An instance of this rule is ved. *újjiti-ṣ*, victory, from *ud-* and *jiti-ṣ*.

§ 51. **Idg. dh.** Idg. *dh* = skr. *dh*.

idg. **dhérsō*: skr. *dhárṣāmi*, I dare, cf. gr. θρασύς, θαρρέω, Θερσίτης, goth. *gadars*.

idg. **dhūmó-s*: skr. *dhūmá-s*, smoke, gr. θυμός, lat. *fūmus*.

idg. **dhəi̯ṓ* (root **dhēi̯-*): skr. *dháyāmi*, I suck, goth. *daddja*, cf. gr. θῆσθαι, θήσατο, lat. *fēlāre*, *fēmina*, ohg. *tāan*. To the same root belongs idg. **dhēlu-s*: ved. *dhārú-ṣ*, sucking, gr. θῆλυς.

idg. **dhidhēmi*: skr. *dádhāmi*, I put (instead of **didhāmi*), gr. τίθημι, cf. ags. *dōn*.

idg. **médhu*: skr. *mádhu*, honey, gr. μέθυ, ohg. *meto*.

idg. **k̑ludhí*: ved. *çrudhí*, hear, imperat. of *çṛṇómi*, I hear, gr. κλύω &c.

idg. **médhi̯o-s*: skr. *mádhya-s*, middle, gr. μέσος, lat. *medius*, goth. *midjis*.

In certain cases *zdh* became *ždh* in Aryan, from which skr. *ḍh* (see § 63).

idg. **mizdhó-*: ved. *mīḍhá-m*, prize, contest, gr. μισθός, cf. goth. *mizdō*.

Idg. *dhn* remained unchanged in Indian:

idg. **bhudhnó-s*: ved. *budhná-s*, bottom, cf. gr. πυθμήν, πύνδαξ, lat. *fundus* and ohg. *bodam*.

When followed by an aspirate, *dh* lost its aspiration:

idg. **dhidhēmi*: skr. *dádhāmi*, I put, gr. τίθημι.

Idg. *dh* + *t* is represented by *ddh*: see § 49.

In many Sanskrit words and forms, when *dh* might be expected, we find however *h*. Instances:

idg. **-dhi*, ved. *-dhi*, *-hi*, skr. *-hi*, suff. 2 pers. sing. imperat. act., gr. -θι.

idg. **-medhai*, **-medhə*: ved. & skr. *-mahe*, *-mahi*, suff. 1 pers. plur. med., avest. *-maidē*, gr. *-μεθα*.

Cf. von Bradke (Zeitschr. der D. Morgenl. Ges. 40, 657 sqq.), who explains such cases by Prācritic influence.

Guttural explosives.

§ 52. **General remarks.** A few years ago only two series of gutturals were assumed, viz. a palatal and a velar series. Bezzenberger (Bezz. Beitr. 16, 234 sqq.) has proved, that there was a third series — different from the palatals and velars —, which may be called the *middle* gutturals. In the western Indogermanic languages, viz. in Greek, Italic, Germanic and Celtic, the velars were labialized and the middle gutturals have fallen together with the palatals. In Aryan, Armenian, Phrygian-Thracian, Albanian and Balto-Slavonic the velars were not labialized, but have fallen together with the middle gutturals: here the palatals were changed to spirants. The velars and middle gutturals being represented in Aryan by *one* series, it is preferable not to separate them in a book on Sanskrit phonetics.

§ 53. **The palatalization-rule.** The palatalization-rule concerns the velars and middle gutturals in general: therefore it is to be treated in a separate paragraph, the more so as the discovery of this rule has had a decisive influence on the modern vowel-theories. It has been the strongest, if not the only argument for adopting, that the multiplicity of vowels in the European languages and in Armenian is more original than the Aryan simplicity.

This rule, which was discovered by several scholars at the same time (see Schmidt, Kuhn's Zeitschr. 25, 1—179), may be formulated as follows:

During the Aryan period, before the change of *ĕ* to *ă*, the gutturals (idg. middle gutturals and velars), were palatalized and changed to palatal affricates, when followed by idg. *ĕ*, *ĭ*, *i̯*, and were preserved as gutturals in any other position (cf. however Meillet, Mém. de la Soc. de Ling. 9, 376 sqq.).

Instances of skr. *c*, *j*, *h* (from *jh*), going back on gutturals before *ĕ*, *ĭ*, *i̯*:

idg. **qe*: skr. *ca*, and, gr. τε, lat. *que*.

idg. **qeru-s*, skr. *carú-ṣ*, kettle, pot, icel. *hverr*.

idg. **qetu̯ōres*: skr. *catvā́ras*, four, goth. *fidwōr*, cf. gr. τέσσαρες, lat. *quatuor*.

idg. **pénqe*: skr. *páñca*, five, gr. πέντε, lat. *quinque*, goth. *fimf*.

idg. **léu̯ketai̯*: skr. *rócate*, shines, pleases, cf. gr. λευκός, lat. *lūcet*, goth. *liuhaþ*.

idg. **ǵéretai̯*: ved. *járate*, crackles, invokes, cf. ohg. *quirit*.

idg. **áu̯ges-*: skr. *ójas*, strength, power, cf. *ugrá-s*, mighty, terrible and lat. *augeō*, goth. *aukan*.

idg. **ǵhénmi*: skr. *hánmi*, I slay, cf. gr. θείνω.

idg. **ǵhéros*: ved. *háras*, heat, gr. θέρος.

idg. **-qiti-s*: skr. *ápa-citi-ṣ*, reward, homage, punishment, gr. ἀπό-τισις, τίσις.

idg. **qid*: skr. *cid*, -cunque, gr. τί, lat. *quid*.

idg. **k̂uki-s*: skr. *çúci-ṣ*, light, clear, pure, cf. *çukrá-s*, clear, bright.

idg. **ki̯éu̯etai̯*: skr. *cyávate*, moves, falls, cf. gr. σεύω.

Instances of gutturals, which were not followed by *ĕ*, *ĭ*, *i̯* and therefore remained unchanged:

idg. **kakŭd-*: skr. *kakút* (*d*), *kakúdmān* (*nt*), top, summit, lat. *cacūmen* (from **cacūdmen*).

idg. **kark-*: skr. *karká-s*, *karkaṭa-s*, crab, gr. καρκίνος, lat. *cancer* (from **carcer* or **carcen*).

idg. *skandṓ: skr. skándāmi, I spring, lat. scandō.

idg. *kālo-s: skr. kāla-s, dark, black, cf. gr. κηλίς (*κᾱλίς), spot, κηλάς (*κᾱλάς), „νεφέλη ἄνυδρος καὶ χειμερινὴ ἡμέρα", lat. cālīgo, mist, darkness.

idg. *kāru-s: ved. kārú-ṣ, praiser, singer, cf. gr. κήρῡξ, dor. κᾱ́ρῡξ.

idg. *qā́setai̯: skr. kā́sate, coughs, cf. ags. hwósta, dutch hoest. That the radical vowel was ā (not ō), is seen from lith. kosėti, to cough.

idg. *égāt: skr. ágāt, went, gr. ἔβη, dor. ἔβᾱ.

idg. *qotero-s: skr. katará-s, who (from two), gr. πότερος, ion. κότερος, goth. hwaþar.

idg. *kókso-s, *kóksā: skr. kákṣa-s, region of the girth, girdle &c., underwood, kákṣā, girdle, circular wall, lat. coxa, mhg. hahse.

idg. *jugó-m: skr. yugá-m, yoke, age, gr. ζυγόν, lat. jugum, goth. juk.

idg. *ghono-s: skr. ghaná-s, slayer (ved.), compact &c., gr. φόνος: skr. hánmi, I slay, gr. θείνω.

idg. *dəlghó-s: skr. dīrghá-s, long, cf. gr. δολιχός.

idg. *gṓu̯-s: skr. gā́u-ṣ, cow, gr. βοῦς &c.

idg. *gərú-s: skr. gurú-ṣ, heavy, important, worthy of honor, cf. gr. βαρύς, goth. kaúrus and lat. gravis.

idg. *gərí-s: skr. girí-ṣ, mountain, cf. lith. giria, forest, oslav. gora, mountain.

idg. *gm̥tó-s: skr. gatá-s, gone, gr. βατός, lat. -ventus.

idg. *i̯ḗqr̥-t: skr. yákr̥t (*yā́kr̥t, cf. avest. yākarĕ), liver, gr. ἧπαρ, lat. jecur.

idg. *kréu̯əs: ved. kravíṣ, raw flesh, gr. κρέας, cf. lat. cruor and ags. hréa, icel. hrár.

idg. *k̂ukró-s, *k̂ukló-s: skr. çukrá-s (very common in Vedic), *çuklá-s*, clear, bright, white, cf. comparat. *çóciyān* (*ṁs*) and *çúci-ṣ*, light, clear, pure.

idg. **ugró-s*: skr. *ugrá-s*, mighty, terrible, cf. comparat. *ójīyān* (*ṁs*), akin to lat. *augeō*, goth. *aukan* &c.

idg. **stighnutai̯*: skr. *stighnuté*, ascends (Dhātup. *āskandane*), cf. gr. *στείχω*, goth. *steiga*.

idg. **peṅqti-s*: skr. *paṅktí-ṣ*, row of five, row, cf. gr. *πέμπτος*.

idg. **siséqti*: ved. *síṣakti*, follows, accompanies, cf. *sácate*, gr. *ἕπεται*, lat. *sequitur*.

§ 54. **Idg. q, k.** In Aryan the idg. *q* and *k* have fallen together. Before palatal vowels and the semivowel *i̯* they were palatalized, in all other cases they are represented by *k*.

Instances of idg. *q*, *k*, skr. *k*:

idg. **qāsetai̯*: skr. *kā́sate*, coughs, cf. ags. *hwósta*.

idg. **qotero-s*: skr. *katará-s*, who (from two), gr. *πότερος*, ion. *κότερος*, goth. *hwaþar*.

idg. **i̯ēqr̥-t*: skr. *yákr̥t* (**yā́kr̥t*), gr. *ἧπαρ*, lat. *jecur*.

idg. **peṅqti-s*: skr. *paṅktí-ṣ*, row of five, row, cf. gr. *πέμπτος*.

idg. **kakŭd-*: skr. *kakút* (*d*), *kakúdmān* (*nt*), top, summit, lat. *cacūmen*.

idg. **kark-*: skr. *karká-s*, *karkaṭa-s*, crab, gr. *καρκίνος*, lat. *cancer*.

idg. **kókso-s*, **kóksā*: skr. *kákṣa-s*, region of the girth &c., *kákṣā*, girdle, circular wall, lat. *coxa*, mhg. *hahse*.

idg. **kréu̯əs*: ved. *kravíṣ*, raw flesh, gr. *κρέας*, cf. lat. *cruor* &c.

Instances of idg. *q*, *k*, skr. *c*:

idg. **qeru-s*: skr. *carú-ṣ*, kettle, pot, icel. *hverr*.

idg. **qetu̯óres*: skr. *catvā́ras*, four, goth. *fidwōr*, cf. gr. *τέσσαρες*, lat. *quatuor*.

idg. **péṅqe*: skr. *páñca*, five, gr. *πέντε*, lat. *quinque*, goth. *fimf*.

idg. **qid*: skr. *cid*, -cunque, gr. τί, lat. *quid*.

idg. **léu̯ketai̯*: skr. *rócate*, shines, pleases, cf. gr. λευκός, lat. *lūcet*, goth. *liuhaþ*.

idg. **k̂uki-s*: skr. *çúci-ṣ*, light, clear, pure, cf. *çukrá-s*, bright, light, clear.

idg. **ki̯éu̯etai̯*: skr. *cyávate*, moves, falls, cf. gr. σεύω.

§ 55. **Idg. qh, kh.** Certain examples of idg. *qh*, *kh* are very rare:

idg. **sqhalṓ*: skr. *skhálāmi*, I stumble, cf. gr. σφάλλω (**sqhl̥i̯ō*)?

idg. **k̂oṅkho-s*: skr. *çaṅkhá-s*, shell, gr. κόγχος, cf. lat. *congius*.

Instances of skr. *kh*, iran. χ:

skr. *khára-*, ass, avest. *χara-*.

skr. *khá-s*, well, avest. *χan-*, *χāo*.

skr. *sákhā*, friend, avest. *haχa*.

In skr. *kumbhá-*, pot, the initial *k* was originally aspirated, cf. avest. *χumba-*. The loss of the *h* was caused by dissimilation.

Concerning the combination *cch* (*ch*) it is not yet certain, whether it should be explained from idg. *skh* before palatal vowels or from idg. *sk̂h*. In the former case *gácchāmi*, *icchámi*, *pr̥cchámi* would have *cch* by analogy, because idg. **g̑m̥skhṓ*, **isskhṓ*, **pr̥k̂skhṓ* would have given **gaskhāmi*, **iṣkhāmi*, **pr̥ṣkhāmi*; the *cch* of *gácchati*, *iccháti*, *pr̥ccháti* regularly would represent the idg. *skh* before idg. *e*: idg. **g̑m̥skhéti*, **isskhéti*, **pr̥k̂skhéti*. In the latter case *gácchāmi*, *icchámi*, *pr̥cchámi* also would be organic forms. Cf. on this question Zubatý, Kuhn's Zeitschr. 31, 9 sqq. and Bartholomae, Studien zur idg. sprachgeschichte 2, 3 sqq. Instances:

skr. *chinádmi*, I cut off, cf. avest. *sid-* (*s* from *sk̂*), gr. σχίζω, lat. *scindō*, lith. *skėdžiu* (lith. idg. *sk*).

skr. *chāyā́*, shade, shadow, cf. pers. *sāya* (*s* from *sk̂*), gr. *σκιά*, oslav. *stěnĭ* from **scěnĭ*, **skěnĭ* (slav. idg. *sk*).

skr. *iccháti*, wishes, cf. avest. *isaiti* (*s* from *sk̂*), lith. *jëszkoti*, oslav. *iskati* (lith. *szk*, slav. *sk*, idg. *sk*), ohg. *eiscōn*.

skr. *gácchati*, goes, cf. avest. *jasaiti* (*s* from *sk̂*), gr. *βάσκω*.

skr. *pṛccháti*, asks, cf. avest. *pĕrĕsaiti* (*s* from *sk̂*), lat. *poscō*, ohg. *forscōn*.

§ 56. **Idg. g̑, g.** In Aryan the idg. *g̑* and *g* have fallen together. Before palatal vowels and the semivowel *i̯* they were palatalized, in all other cases they are represented by *g*.

Instances of idg. *g̑*, *g*, skr. *g*:

idg. **g̑ōu̯-s*: skr. *gā́u-ṣ*, cow, gr. *βοῦς* &c.

idg. **g̑ərú-s*: skr. *gurú-ṣ*, heavy, cf. gr. *βαρύς*, goth. *kaúrus* (and lat. *gravis*).

idg. **ég̑āt*: skr. *ágāt*, went, gr. *ἔβη*.

idg. **g̑m̥tó-s*: skr. *gatá-s*, gone, gr. *βατός*, lat. *-ventus*.

idg. **jugó-m*: skr. *yugá-m*, yoke, age, gr. *ζυγόν*, lat. *jugum*, goth. *juk*.

idg. **ugró-s*: skr. *ugrá-s*, mighty, terrible, cf. lat. *augeō*, goth. *aukan*.

Instances of idg. *g̑*, *g*, skr. *j*:

idg. **g̑éretai̯*: ved. *járate*, crackles, invokes, cf. ohg. *quirit*.

idg. **au̯ges-*: skr. *ójas-*, strength, power, cf. *ugrá-s*, mighty, terrible, lat. *augeō*, goth. *aukan*.

§ 57. **Idg. g̑h, gh.** In Aryan the idg. *g̑h* and *gh* have fallen together. Before palatal vowels and the semivowel *i̯* they became *jh*, in all other cases they are represented by *gh*. In Indian *jh* became *h*.

Instances of idg. *g̑h*, *gh*, skr. *gh*:

idg. **g̑hono-s*: skr. *ghaná-s*, slayer (ved.), compact &c., gr. *φόνος*, cf. ohg. *gundea*, ags. *gúð*.

idg. **dəlghó-s*: skr. *dīrghá-s*, long, cf. gr. δολιχός.

idg. **stighnutai̯*: skr. *stighnuté*, ascends, cf. gr. στείχω, goth. *steiga*.

Instances of idg. *g̑h*, *gh*, skr. *h*:

idg. **g̑hénmi*: skr. *hánmi*, I slay, cf. gr. θείνω.

idg. **g̑héros*: ved. *háras*, heat, gr. θέρος.

idg. **dhrughes*: ved. *drúhas*, harming spirits, cf. skr. *drúhyāmi*, I harm, avest. *druj-*, ohg. *triogan*.

When followed by an aspirate, *gh* (*jh*) lost its aspiration:

idg. **ghr̥dhi̯ō*: skr. *gŕ̥dhyāmi*, I am eager, cf. goth. *grēdus*, *grēdags*.

idg. **g̑heg̑hóna*: skr. *jaghána*, I have slain: *hánmi*, I slay, gr. θείνω.

Idg. *g̑h* + *t* and *gh* + *t* are represented by *gdh*: see § 49.

Palatal explosives.

§ 58. **General remarks.** Besides the velars and middle gutturals there was a third series of guttural explosives, formed at the foremost part of the hard palate. These foremost gutturals are called palatals. In Aryan, Armenian, Phrygian-Thracian, Albanian and Balto-Slavonic the palatal explosives were changed to palatal spirants: in the same dialect-groups the velars and middle gutturals fell together into one series of guttural explosives. In Greek, Italic, Germanic and Celtic, where the velars were labialized, the palatals fell together with the middle gutturals. According to the manner, in which the gutturals were treated, the Indogermanic languages may be divided into two groups, a western, where the difference between palatals and middle gutturals has been effaced, and an eastern, where the velars have fallen together with the middle gutturals, but where the palatal explosives have become spirants. Von Bradke has called the western group that of the *centum*-languages, the eastern group that of the *satĕm*-languages. It may be supposed, that the *centum*-languages descend from an other dialect of the mother-tongue than the *satĕm*-languages. Cf. von Bradke, Ueber methode und ergebnisse der arischen alterthumswissenschaft (Giessen 1890), 63.

§ 59. **Idg. k̑.** During the Aryan period the idg. *k̑* became *ç*. This voiceless palatal spirant remained unchanged in Indian:

idg. **k̑m̥tó-m*: skr. *çatá-m*, hundred, gr. ἑ-κατόν, lat. *centum*, goth. *hund*, lith. *szimtas* (cf. § 18).

idg. **k̑aṅkú-s*: skr. *çaṅkú-ṣ*, wedge, stake, oslav. *sąkŭ*, branch, cf. skr. *çā́khā*, branch, lith. *szaka* (also goth. *hōha?*).

idg. **k̑énsō*: skr. *çáṁsāmi*, I recite, I praise, I announce, cf. lat. *censeō*.

idg. **k̑ūro-s*: skr. *çū́ra-s*, mighty, bold, hero, gr. -κῦρος in ἄ-κῡρος, not valid.

idg. **k̑u̯ō(n)*: skr. *çvā́ (n)*, dog, lith. *szů*, with *n* gr. κύων, cf. goth. *hunds*.

idg. **su̯ek̑uro-s*: skr. *çváçura-s*, father in law, gr. ἑκυρός, cf. lat. *socer* and goth. *swaíhra*. Oslav. *svekrŭ* has idg. *k* or *q*; on the contrary lith. *szeszuras* regularly has *sz* from *k̑*. The feminine of **su̯ek̑uro-s* is **su̯ek̑rū́-s*: skr. *çvaçrū́-ṣ*, mother in law, lat. *socrus*, oslav. *svekry* (with *k* as *svekrŭ*), cf. gr. ἑκυρά (probably an analogous formation to ἑκυρός) and goth. *swaíhrō*.

idg. **u̯ói̯k̑o-s*: skr. *veça-s*, house, gr. οἶκος, lat. *vīcus*, cf. goth. *weihs*.

idg. **dn̥k̑ō*: skr. *dáçāmi*, I bite, cf. gr. δάκνω (also ohg. *zangar*, sharp).

idg. **ák̑ru*: skr. *áçru*, tear, cf. *açrá-m* (of course to be written with *ç*, not with *s*), tear, lith. *aszara* (with an initial *d* gr. δάκρυ, lat. *lacruma*, goth. *tagr*).

idg. **a͡kmō(n)*: ved. *áçmā* (*n*), stone, gr. ἄκμων, lith. pl. tantum *aszmens*, edge, but with *k* or *q* lith. *akmů*, oslav. *kamy*, stone (cf. ohg. *hamar*, icel. *hamarr*, originally, „a weapon of stone"?).

idg. **dedórk͡a*: skr. *dadárça*, I have seen, gr. δέδορκα.

The idg. combination *k͡t* regularly became *çt* in Aryan, that is represented in Indian by *ṣṭ*:

idg. **ok͡tō(u̯)*: skr. *aṣṭā́* (ved.), *aṣṭā́u*, eight, gr. ὀκτώ, lat. *octō*, goth. *ahtau*.

idg. **dik͡ti-s*: skr. *diṣṭi-ṣ*, indication, prescription, destiny, ohg. *-ziht* in *inziht*, accusation, cf. lat. *dictiō* and with strong vocalism gr. δεῖξις.

idg. **u̯ék͡ti*: skr. *váṣṭi*, is willing, cf. *uçánt-*, willing, gr. ἑκών. The first person is *váçmi* from **u̯ék͡mi*.

Brugmann 1, 299 assumes, that *sk͡* became *cch* (*ch*) in Indian: cf. however § 55 and § 62.

The idg. combination *k͡s* is represented by *kṣ*:

idg. **u̯ék͡si*: skr. *vákṣi*, thou art willing, cf. *váçmi*, I am willing, gr. ἑκών.

idg. **dék͡sino-s*: skr. *dákṣiṇa-s*, right, southern, clever, able, oslav. *desĭnŭ*, lith. *deszinė* (fem. of the *ė*-class, right hand), cf. gr. δεξιός, lat. *dexter*, goth. *taíhswa*.

§ 60. **Idg. ĝ.** During the Aryan period the idg. *ĝ* became a voiced palatal spirant (*ž*), which was changed in Indian to an affricate (*dž*, written *j*):

idg. **ĝénos*: ved. *jánas*, race, family, gr. γένος, lat. *genus*, cf. goth. *kuni*: skr. *janáyāmi*, I beget, I produce, gr. γίγνομαι, lat. *gignō* &c. Avest. *zan-* proves, that the *j* of *janáyāmi* is an idg. *ĝ*.

idg. **ĝónu*: skr. *jā́nu*, knee, cf. gr. γόνυ, lat. *genu* and with loss of the root-vowel ved. *jñu-* in *jñu-bā́dh-*, bending the knees, gr. *γνυ-* in *γνυπετεῖν*, goth. *kniu*. Avest. *zanva*, knees.

idg. **ĝnōtó-s*: skr. *jñātá-s*, known, gr. *γνωτός*, lat. *nōtus*: skr. *jānā́mi*, I know, gr. *γιγνώσκω*, lat. *nōscō* (*gnōscō*), cf. ags. *cnáwan*, ohg. *chnāan* (with idg. *ē*) and ohg. *einchnuadil, cnuodelen*. That we have to do with idg. *ĝ*, appears from lith. *žinoti*, oslav. *znati* &c.

idg. **ĝusó*: skr. *juṣā́mi*, I take pleasure, I relish, cf. idg. **ĝéu̯sō*, gr. *γεύω*, goth. *kiusa* and idg. **ĝustu-s*, lat. *gustus*, goth. *kustus*. Avest. *zaoša-* (= skr. *jóṣa-*), wish.

idg. **bhərĝo-s*: skr. *bhūrja-s*, birch, cf. ohg. *pirihha*. The *ĝ* appears from oslav. *brěza*, lith. *beržas*.

idg. **mr̥ĝó*: skr. *mr̥jā́mi*, I rub, wipe, strip, cf. gr. *ἀμέλγω*, lat. *mulgeō*, ohg. *milchu* &c. Lith. *melžu*, oslav. *mlŭzą* prove, that we have *ĝ*.

The idg. combination *ĝb(h)* regularly became in Aryan *žb(h)*, from which skr. *ḍb(h)*: cf. § 63. Example:

idg. **u̯iĝbhís*: skr. *viḍbhíṣ*, instrum. pl. of *viç-*, nom. *viṭ*, settlement, community, clan, tribe, people, cf. gr. *οἶκος*, lat. *vīcus* &c.

§ 61. **Idg. ĝh.** During the Aryan period the idg. *ĝh* became *žh*. This aspirated spirant is in general represented by skr. *h*. The intermediate *jh* is preserved in skr. *ujjhitá-s*, left, from **ud-jhita-s*: *jáhāmi*, I leave (*ujjhāmi* has been formed by analogy). Instances of idg. *ĝh*, skr. *h*:

idg. **ĝhéi̯men-*: ved. *héman-*, winter, gr. *χεῖμα*, *χειμών*, cf. skr. *himá-m*, snow, gr. *χιών*, lat. *hiems*. The *ĝh* appears from lith. *žëma*, oslav. *zima* &c.

idg. **ĝhansó-s*: skr. *haṁsá-s*, goose, swan, cf. gr. *χήν*, lat. *anser*, ohg. *gans*. Lith. *žąsis* proves, that we have *ĝh*; surprising is the *g* of oslav. *gąsĭ* (perhaps an ancient loan from Germanic).

idg. *léi̯ĝhmi: skr. léhmi, I lick, cf. gr. λείχω, lat. lingō, goth. -laigōn. The ĝh appears from lith. lëžiu, oslav. ližą &c.

idg. *bhāĝhu-s: skr. bāhú-ṣ, arm, gr. πῆχυς, ohg. buog. Avest. bāzu-.

idg. *u̯éĝhō: skr. váhāmi, I carry, lat. vehō, goth. -wiga. Lith. vežu, oslav. vezą &c. prove, that we have to do with ĝh.

Idg. ĝh + t became skr. ḍh, sometimes with modification of a preceding vowel:

idg. *léi̯ĝh-ti: skr. léḍhi, licks, cf. gr. λείχω.

idg. *liĝh-tós: skr. līḍhá-s, licked: léḍhi.

idg. *uĝh-tó-s: skr. ūḍhá-s, carried: váhāmi, I carry.

idg. *dhr̥ĝh-tó-s: skr. dr̥ḍhá-s, firm: dŕ̥hyāmi, dŕ̥ṁhāmi, I make firm.

idg. *sēĝh-tó-s: skr. sāḍhá-s, overpowered &c.: sáhāmi, I overpower, I withstand &c., gr. ἔχω.

idg. *u̯éĝh-tum: skr. vóḍhum, to carry: váhāmi, I carry.

idg. *séĝh-tum: skr. sóḍhum, to withstand &c.: sáhami, I withstand &c.

When followed by an aspirate, ĝh became j:

idg. *ĝhiĝhāmi: skr. jáhāmi, I leave. The i of the reduplication-syllable was replaced by a before the end of the Aryan period, cf. avest. zazāiti, leaves.

Spirants.

§ 62. **Idg. s.** In general the idg. s remained unchanged:

idg. *septn̥: skr. saptá, seven, gr. ἑπτά, lat. septem, cf. goth. sibun. Lith. septyni proves, that we have to do with n̥, not with m̥.

idg. *séno-s: ved. sána-s, old, gr. fem. ἕνη, cf. lat. senex, goth. sineigs.

idg. **sréu̯ō*: skr. *srávāmi*, I flow, I stream, gr. *ῥέω*, cf. ohg. *stroum*.

idg. **véstai̯*: skr. *váste*, clothes one's self, puts on, cf. *vásana-m*, *vástra-m*, garment, gr. *ἕννυμι*, *ἑανός*, *ἐσθής*, lat. *vestis*, goth. *wasjan*, *wasti*.

idg. **dōsi̯ō*: skr. *dāsyámi*, gr. *δώσω*.

idg. **ĝénos*, gen. **ĝénesos*: ved. *jánas*, gen. *jánasas*, race, family, gr. *γένος*, lat. *genus*.

idg. **ék̂u̯o-s*: skr. *áçva-s*, horse, gr. *ἵππος*, lat. *equus*, germ. **éχwoz*, icel. *jór*, ags. *eoh*.

Already during the Aryan period *s* was changed to *ś* after *ĭ*, *ŭ*, *i̯*, *u̯*, *r̥*, *r*, *q*, *k*, *k̂*. In the same conditions *ss* became *śś*. In Indian the *ś* is lingualized and *śś* has become *kṣ* (cf. however Wackernagel 1, 137). I can not agree with Hirt (Idg. forschungen 4, 44), Zubatý (Arch. f. slav. phil. 16, 404 note), Pedersen (Idg. forschungen 5, 33 sqq.) and Wackernagel 1, 231, who assume a connection between the Aryan change of *s* to *ś* and the Slavonic transition of *s* to *ch* (see Arch. f. slav. phil. 16, 368 sqq.; Museum 4, 50).

idg. **sthisthāmi*: skr. *tíṣṭhāmi*, I stand, gr. *ἵστημι*, cf. lat. *sistō*.

idg. **ustó-s*: skr. *uṣṭá-s*, burned, lat. *ustus*.

idg. **u̯ĺ̥qoi̯su*: skr. *vŕ̥keṣu*, loc. plur. of *vŕ̥ka-s*, wolf, oslav. *vlŭcěchŭ*.

idg. **ĝeu̯ster-*: ved. *joṣṭár-*, *jóṣṭar-*, loving, cf. gr. *γευστήριον*.

idg. **du̯éi̯ssi*: skr. *dvékṣi* (from **dvái̯śśi*), thou hatest, 2 pers. of *dvéṣmi*.

idg. **sau̯ssi̯ō*: skr. *çokṣyámi* (from **sau̯śśyámi*), I shall dry up, gr. *αὔσω*.

idg. **dhr̥snéu̯mi*, **dhérsō*: skr. *dhr̥ṣṇómi*, *dhárṣāmi*, I dare, cf. gr. *θαρρέω* &c.

idg. **kərs-*: skr. *çīrṣá-m*, *çīrṣán-*, head, cf. *çíras*, head, gr. *κόρση* (*κόρρη*), *κέρας*, *κάρᾱ*, lat. *cerebrum*, *cernuus*, icel. *hjarne*, *hjarse*, ohg. *hirni*.

idg. **u̯ersā*: skr. *varṣá*, rain, gr. *ἕρση*, *ἔρση*.

idg. **u̯eqsi̯ō*: skr. *vakṣyámi*, I shall say: *vácmi*, I say, cf. *vák*, voice, lat. *vōx* &c.

idg. **dheksi̯ō*: skr. *dhakṣyámi*, I shall burn: *dáhāmi*, I burn, lith. *degu*, cf. goth. *dags*.

idg. **u̯ék̂si*: skr. *vákṣi*, thou art willing, cf. *váçmi*, I am willing, gr. *ἑκών*.

It is to be noticed, that skr. *ṣ* was turned back into *s*, when immediately followed by *r̥* or *r*:

idg. **tisres*, **tisr̥bhis* &c.: skr. *tisrás*, fem. three, instrum. *tisŕ̥bhiṣ*, cf. avest. *tis̆arō*, irish *teora*.

Brugmann 1, 412 and Bartholomae (Studien zur idg. sprachgeschichte 2, 5) assume, that the idg. *sq*, *sk* before palatal vowels became *çc* in Aryan, cf. ved. *paçcá*, behind, later, west, avest. *pasca* (originally an instrumental, ending in idg. *ē*). Against this opinion Meillet, Mém. de la Soc. de Ling. 9, 375 sq.

It would seem, that the idg. *sqh*, *skh* before palatal vowels are represented in Indian by *cch* (*ch*), but Bartholomae (Studien zur idg. sprachgeschichte 2, 3 sqq.) has tried to prove, that *cch* (*ch*) goes back on a combination of *k̂*. Cf. § 55, where examples of *cch* are given.

The idg. *ss* after *a*-vowels became *ts* in Indian. In most cases however *ss* had been simplified before the end of the Indogermanic period, cf. skr. *ási*, thou art, avest. *ahi*, gr. *εἶ*, idg. **ési* from **és-si*. Instances of idg. *ss*, skr. *ts*:

idg. **vessi̯ō*: skr. *vatsyámi*, I shall put on, gr. *ἕσσω*, fut. of idg. **ves-*.

idg. *u̯essi̯ō: skr. *vatsyā́mi*, I shall dwell, fut. of *vásāmi*, I dwell, goth. *wisan*.

idg. *u̯idu̯éssu: skr. *vidvátsu*, loc. pl. of *vidvā́n*, knowing, wise, cf. gr. εἰδώς and goth. *weitwōþs*.

Between explosives *s* was lost: *utthā́tum*, to stand up, to rise up, from **utsthā́tum* (*ud* + *sthā́tum*); *átāpta*, you were warm, from **átāpsta* (aor. of *tápāmi*).

In the neighbourhood of *ç* and *ṣ* the idg. *s* became assimilated to *ç*:

idg. **su̯eḱuro-s*: skr. *çváçura-s*, father in law, gr. ἑκυρός, cf. with a similar assimilation lith. *szeszuras*.

idg. **smaḱru*: skr. *çmáçru*, beard, cf. lith. *smakra*, chin (with idg. *k*), and perhaps lat. *maxilla*.

idg. **suskó-s*: skr. *çuṣká-s*, dry, avest. *huška-*, cf. lith. *sausas*, oslav. *suchŭ*, ohg. *sōr*.

idg. **ḱasó-s*: skr. *çaçá-s*, hare, cf. ohg. *haso*, ags. *hara*, opruss. *sasnis*.

§ 63. **Idg. z.** Osthoff (Kuhn's Zeitschr. 23, 87—89) has proved, that during the Indogermanic period *s* before voiced consonants had become voiced. In Aryan this voiced sibilant (*z*) was preserved after *a*-vowels, but changed to *ž* after *ĭ*, *ŭ*, *i̯*, *u̯*. In Indian the *ž* became lingual. Afterwards it disappeared in any position, as well as the unchanged *z*.

Idg. *azd(h)*, *ezd(h)*, *ozd(h)* = ar. *azd(h)* = skr. *ed(h)*:

idg. **sezdi̯ḗt*: ved. *sedyā́t*, 3 pers. sing. optat. perf. of the root *sad-*, to sit, avest. *hazdyāþ*.

idg. **ezdhí*, **zdhi*: skr. *edhí*, imperat. of the root *as-*, to be, avest. *zdī*, cf. gr. ἴσθι.

Idg. *āzd(h)*, *ēzd(h)*, *ōzd(h)* = ar. *āzd(h)* = skr. *ād(h)*:

idg. **ēzdhu̯ai̯*: skr. *ā́dhve*, you sit, cf. *ā́ste*, sits, gr. ἧσται.

idg. *$\hat{k}$ăzdhí: skr. *çādhí*, imperat. of the root *çās-*, to rule, to punish &c.

Idg. *zd(h)* after *ĭ*, *ŭ*, *i̯*, *u̯* = ar. *żd(h)* = skr. *ḍ(h)*:

idg. **nizdó-s*: skr. *nīḍá-s*, nest, lat. *nīdus*, ohg. *nest*.

idg. **duzdê̂k-*: ved. *dūḍā́ç-*, not pious, cf. skr. *duṣ-*, gr. δυς-, goth. *tuz-*.

idg. **éstau̯zdhu̯am*: ved. *ástoḍhvam*, 2 pers. plur. aor. med. of *stáumi*, I praise.

Idg. *zb(h)* after *a*-vowels = ar. *zb(h)* = skr. *db(h)*:

idg. **u̯idu̯ezbhis*: skr. *vidvádbhiṣ*, instrum. pl. of *vidvā́n*, knowing.

idg. **mēzbhis*: ved. *mādbhíṣ*, instrum. pl. of *mā́s*, moon, month.

Idg. *zb(h)* after *ĭ*, *ŭ*, *i̯*, *u̯* = ar. *żb(h)* = *ḍb(h)*:

idg. **du̯izbhís*: skr. *dviḍbhíṣ*, instrum. pl. of *dviṣ-*, nom. *dviṭ*, hating.

idg. **u̯ipruzbhís*: skr. *vipruḍbhiṣ*, instrum. pl. of *viprúṣ-*, nom. *viprúṭ*, crumb, spot, spark.

Idg. *zg(h)* after *a*-vowels, not followed by a palatal vowel or *i̯*, = ar. *zg(h)* = skr. *dg(h)*:

idg. **mezgú-s*: skr. *madgú-ṣ*, a kind of waterfowl, cf. lat. *mergus*: skr. *májjati*, see below.

Idg. *zg* after *a*-vowels, followed by a palatal vowel, = ar. *zj* (*zdž*) = skr. *jj*:

idg. **mézgeti*: skr. *májjati*, sinks under, dives, lat. *mergit*.

Between explosives *z* is lost in Indian: ved. *ámugdhvam* from **ámugzdhvam*, 2 pers. pl. aor. med. of *muñcáti*, releases, loosens.

§ 64. **Idg. j.** The idg. spirant *j* has fallen together with the semivowel *i̯* in all Indogermanic languages except Greek:

idg. **jugó-m*: skr. *yugá-m*, yoke, gr. ζυγόν, lat. *jugum*, goth. *juk*.

idg. **jéső*: skr. *yásāmi* (the common form in literature is *yásyāmi*), I seethe, I boil, gr. ζέω, cf. obg. *jesan*.

idg. **jéu̯o-s*: skr. *yáva-s*, corn, barley, cf. gr. ζειαί, spelt, lith. *javai*, corn.

idg. **jūs-*: ved. *yū́ṣ-*, *yūṣán-*, skr. *yūṣa-s*, *yūṣa-m*, broth, lat. *jūs*, oslav. *jucha*, cf. gr. ζύμη.

Perhaps also:

idg. **k̑éjtai̯*: skr. *çéte*, lies, gr. κεῖται.

idg. **tjeg̑-*: skr. *tyájāmi*, I leave, *tyaktá-s*, left, gr. σέβομαι, σεπτός.

See Brugmann 1, 454. If *çéte* and *tyájāmi* originally contained the semivowel *i̯*, a gradation *çe-*: **çi-*, *tyaj-*: **tij-* might have been expected.

§ 65. **Idg. v.** The mother-language seems to have possessed a spirant *v*, which already in Aryan had fallen together with the semivowel *u̯*. The most certain criterion of idg. *v* is the absence of weaker forms containing *u* (Brugmann, 1, 409). Instance:

idg. **véstai̯*: skr. *váste*, clothes one's self, puts on, cf. *vásana-m*, *vásma* (*n*), *vástra-m*, garment, gr. ἕννυμι, ἑανός, εἷμα (lesb. Ϝέμμα), ἐσθής, lat. *vestis*, *vestiō*, goth. *wasjan*, *wasti*.

§ 66. **Idg. γ.** Von Fierlinger (Kuhn's Zeitschr. 27, 478 note) supposes, that there was a voiced palatal spirant γ in the mother-language, represented by skr. *h*, avest. *z*, gr. γ, lat. *g*, germ. *k*. Though this theory may not claim a high degree of probability, it will be useful to mention the few cases, where skr. *h* seems to correspond to gr. γ &c.:

idg. **γénu-s*: skr. *hánu-ṣ*, jaw, gr. γένυς, cf. goth. *kinnus* and lat. *gena*.

idg. **γe*: skr. *ha*, enclit. particle, gr. γε, goth. *-k* in *mik*, *þuk*, *sik*.

idg. **γosto-s*, **əγosto-s*: skr. *hásta-s*, hand, trunk (of an elephant), paw &c., gr. ἀγοστός (see de Saussure 53).

idg. **eγŏm*: skr. *ahám*, I, gr. ἐγών, cf. gr. ἐγώ, lat. *ego*, goth. *ik*.

idg. **dhuγətē(r)*: skr. *duhitā́ (r)*, daughter, gr. θυγάτηρ, cf. goth. *daúhtar*.

idg. **gŭγ-*: skr. *gúhāmi*, I hide, cf. Ὠγυγία, Ὤγυγος, Γύγης.

idg. **meγ-*: skr. *mahā́n (nt)*, great, cf. ved. *máhi*, nom. acc. neutr. great, adv. very, subst. greatness, gr. μέγα (idg. **méγə*).

§ 67. **Idg.** *þ*, *đ*. In general skr. *kṣ* corresponds to gr. ξ, but in some cases we find gr. κτ, χθ or φθ instead of ξ. We must assume, that the skr. *ṣ*, which is represented by gr. τ, θ, goes back on dental sounds, which were different from *s* and from the ordinary idg. dental explosives. Perhaps these dental sounds were spirants (*þ*, *đ*). See Brugmann 1, 409 sq. and Kretschmer, Kuhn's Zeitschr. 31, 429 sqq.

Instances of skr. *kṣ*, gr. κτ, idg. *kþ*, *k̑þ*:

ved. *kṣémi*, I dwell, skr. *kṣétra-m*, field, *kṣití-ṣ*, dwelling, abode, earth, ved. pl. tribes, gr. rhod. κτοίνα, dwelling-place, gr. κτίζω, κτίσις, ἀμφικτίονες, ἐϋκτίμενος. Avest. *šaeiti* proves, that the initial guttural was *k̑*.

ved. *kṣáyāmi*, I possess, gr. κτάομαι, κτῆμα. Avest. *χšayeiti* proves, that the original *anlaut* was *k*.

skr. *kṣaṇómi*, I hurt, gr. κτείνω. Opers. *-χšata-* = skr. *kṣatá-*.

skr. *ṛ́kṣa-s*, bear, gr. ἄρκτος, lat. *ursus*. Avest. *arĕša-* (?).

skr. *tákṣā (n)*, carpenter, gr. τέκτων, cf. lat. *texere*. Avest. *taš-*.

Instance of skr. *kṣ*, gr. φθ, idg. *qþh*:

skr. *kṣiṇā́mi* (ved.), later *kṣiṇómi*, *kṣáyāmi*, I destroy, *kṣíti-ṣ*, destruction, gr. φθίνω, φθίσις. Avest. *χšaya-* proves, that skr. *kṣ*, gr. *φθ* here goes back on a combination of voiceless consonants.

Instances of skr. *kṣ*, gr. *χθ*, *φθ*, idg. *ĝđh*, *g̑đh*:

ved. *kṣá-s*, dwelling-place, earth, pl. *kṣámas*, gr. *χθών*, cf. gr. *χαμαί*, lat. *humus*, avest. *zěm-*, lith. *žemė*, oslav. *zemlja*, which prove, that skr. *kṣ*, gr. *χθ* here represents an idg. combination of voiced consonants.

skr. *kṣárāmi*, I flow, melt away, perish, gr. *φθείρω*. Avest. *γžaraiti* proves, that the initial group of consonants was originally voiced.

B. The relation of the Indian consonants to the Indogermanic.

Semivowels.

§ 68. **Skr. y.** In skr. *y* have fallen together the idg. *i̯* and *j*.

Skr. *y* = idg. *i̯*:

skr. *yá-s*, who, gr. *ὅς*.

skr. *yákṛt*, liver, originally **yắkṛt*, gr. *ἧπαρ*, lat. *jecur*.

skr. *tráyas*, three, gr. *τρεῖς*, lat. *trēs*, goth. *þreis*.

skr. *mádhya-s*, middle, gr. *μέσος*, lat. *medius*, goth. *midjis*.

skr. *jyā́*, bowstring, cf. gr. *βιός*.

Skr. *y* = idg. *j*:

skr. *yugá-m*, yoke, gr. *ζυγόν*, lat. *jugum*, goth. *juk*.

skr. *yásāmi* (*yásyāmi*), I seethe, I boil, gr. *ζέω*, cf. ohg. *jesan*.

skr. *yáva-s*, corn, barley, cf. gr. *ζειαί*, lith. *javai*.

skr. *tyájāmi*, I leave, cf. gr. *σέβομαι*, *σεμνός*.

§ 69. **Skr. v.** In skr. *v* have fallen together the idg. *u̯* and *v*.

Skr. *v* = idg. *u̯*:

skr. *vácas*, word, *vák*, voice, gr. ἔπος, lat. *vōx*.

skr. *véda*, I know, gr. οἶδα, goth. *wait*.

skr. *veça-s*, house, gr. οἶκος, lat. *vīcus*, cf. goth. *weihs*.

skr. *náva-s*, new, gr. νέος, lat. *novus*, cf. ved. *návya-s*, goth. *niujis* &c.

skr. *svādú-ṣ*, sweet, gr. ἡδύς, cf. lat. *suāvis* and os. *swōti*.

skr. *sárva-s*, all, gr. ὅλος, οὖλος.

Skr. *v* = idg. *v*:

skr. *váste*, puts on, cf. gr. ἕννῡμι, ἐσθής, lat. *vestis*, goth. *wasjan*.

Nasals.

§ 70. **Skr. m.** Skr. *m* = idg. *m*:

skr. *mātá*, mother, gr. μήτηρ, lat. *māter*, ohg. *muoter*.

skr. *mṛti-ṣ*, death, lat. *mors*, cf. goth. *maúrþr*.

skr. *mnāta-s*, mentioned, cf. gr. μιμνήσκω.

skr. *mláyāmi*, I wither, cf. gr. βλᾱ́ξ.

skr. *vámāmi*, *vámimi*, I vomit, cf. gr. ἐμέω, lat. *vomō*.

skr. *smáyate*, smiles, cf. gr. Φιλομμειδής, μειδιάω, lat. *mīrus*, engl. *smile*.

skr. *gharmá-s*, heat, lat. *formus*, ohg. *warm*, cf. gr. θερμός.

ved. *jámbha-s*, set of teeth, tooth, gr. γόμφος, ohg. *chamb*.

skr. *tám*, acc. pron., gr. τόν, lat. *is-tum*, goth. *þan-a*.

§ 71. **Skr. n.** Skr. *n* = idg. *n*:

skr. *náu-ṣ*, ship, gr. ναῦς, cf. lat. *nāvis*, icel. *nó-*.

skr. *nábhas*, sky, gr. νέφος, cf. gr. νεφέλη, lat. *nebula*, ohg. *nebul*.

skr. *nāma (n)*, name, lat. *nōmen*, cf. gr. ὄνομα and goth. *namō*.

ved. *sána-s*, old, gr. fem. ἕνη, cf. lat. *senex* and goth. *sineigs*.

ved. *vidmáne*, to know, gr. ἴδμεναι.

skr. voc. *tákṣan*, carpenter, gr. τέκτον.

In some cases the skr. *n* goes back on idg. *m*:

ved. *gántu*, 3 pers. sing. imperat. of *gam-*, to go. Idg. *mt* became *nt*.

ved. *dán*, of the house, gr. δεσ- in δεσπότης, cf. ved. *dáma-s*, gr. δόμος &c. At the end of words idg. *ms* became *n*.

§ 72. **Skr. ṇ.** Skr. *ṇ* often goes back on idg. *n*: in most cases the lingualization is due to the influence of neighbouring lingual consonants. In an other group of words *ṇ* is the representative of idg. *ln*.

Skr. *ṇ* = idg. *n*:

skr. *kṛṣṇá-s*, black, opruss. *kirsna-*.

skr. *uṣṇá-s*, hot: *óṣāmi*, gr. εὕω, lat. *ūrō*.

ved. *mṛṇámi*, I crush, gr. med. μάρναμαι.

skr. *tṛ́ṇa-m*, grass, cf. goth. *þaúrnus*.

skr. *dvéṣāṇi*, 1 pers. sing. praes. conj. (imperat.) of *dvéṣmi*, I hate.

skr. *krīṇámi*, I buy, cf. gr. ἐπριάμην.

In loans from Prākrit dialects, not in the neighbourhood of linguals:

skr. *maṇí-ṣ*, jewel, os. *meni*, cf. lat. *monīle*.

skr. *bhaṇāmi*, I speak, ved. *bhánāmi*.

Skr. *ṇ* = idg. *ln*:

skr. *kiṇa-s*, callosity, lat. *callus* (*callum*).

skr. *kuṇi-ṣ*, lame of one arm, cf. gr. κυλλός.

skr. *āṇí-ṣ*, the leg immediately above the knee, linch-pin, cf. gr. ὠλένη, lat. *ulna* and goth. *aleina*.

skr. *pāṇí-ṣ*, hand, cf. gr. παλάμη, lat. *palma*, ags. *folm*.

In loans from Prākrit dialects *ṇ* may represent the idg. combination *rn*:

skr. *gaṇá-s*, troop, cf. gr. *ἀγείρω*.

§ 73. **Skr. ṅ.** Skr. *ṅ* = idg. *ṅ*:

skr. *aṅká-s*, lap, hook, gr. *ὄγκος*, lat. *uncus*.

skr. *bhaṅgá-s*, wave, cf. lith. *banga*.

§ 74. **Skr. ñ.** Before palatal affricates, which represent idg. velars or middle gutturals, skr. *ñ* goes back on idg. *ṅ*. Before *j*, idg. *ĝ* the *ñ* is original.

Skr. *ñ* = idg. *ṅ*:

skr. *páñca*, five, gr. *πέντε*, lat. *quinque*, goth. *fimf*.

§ 75. **Nasalization of vowels.** The nasalization of vowels is a remainder of idg. nasals. In Sanskrit all nasals before original or secondary spirants were reduced to anusvāra:

skr. *áṁsa-s*, shoulder, goth. *ams*, cf. gr. *ὦμος* and lat. *umerus*.

skr. *haṁsá-s*, goose, swan &c., cf. gr. *χήν*, ohg. *gans* and lat. *anser*.

skr. *ānáṁça*, perf. of *açnómi*, I attain, *áṁça-s*, portion, part, cf. gr. *ἤνεγκον*, lat. *nanciscor*.

ved. *áṁhas*, distress, lat. *angus-* in *angustus*, cf. gr. *ἄγχω*, lat. *angō* and goth. *aggwus*.

Liquids.

§ 76. **Skr. r.** Skr. *r* regularly corresponds to idg. *r*, but in many cases it goes back on idg. *l*.

Skr. *r* = idg. *r*:

skr. *rájyāmi*, I am (get) red, affected with a strong feeling, gr. *ῥέζω*.

skr. *rá-s*, riches, wealth, lat. *rēs*.

skr. *rā́ṭ* (**rāk* from **rākṣ*), king, lat. *rēx*.

skr. *bhárāmi*, I bear, gr. *φέρω*, lat. *ferō*, goth. *baíra*.

skr. *pári*, around, gr. *πέρι*, lat. *per*, goth. *faír-*.

skr. *smárāmi*, I remember, cf. lat. *memor*.

skr. voc. *mā́tar*, mother, gr. *μῆτερ*.

Skr. *r* = idg. *l*:

skr. *riréca*, I left, gr. *λέλοιπα*, goth. *laihw*.

skr. *rákṣāmi*, I protect, cf. gr. *ἀλέξω*.

ved. *rámbate*, hangs down, skr. *lámbate* (already Çat. Br.), cf. lat. *lābor*.

ved. *réhmi*, I lick, skr. *léhmi*, cf. gr. *λείχω*, lat. *lingō*, goth. *-laigōn*.

About the relation of the Vedic dialect to Sanskrit (the Brāhmaṇa's and the epic poems included) see § 43.

§ 77. **Skr. l.** Skr. *l* regularly corresponds to idg. *l*:

skr. *lámbate*, hangs down, cf. lat. *lābor*.

skr. *léhmi*, I lick, cf. gr. *λείχω* &c.

skr. *limpámi*, I smear, cf. gr. *λίπος*, *λιπαρός* &c.

skr. *lúbhyāmi*, I desire, cf. lat. *lubet*, goth. *liufs*.

skr. *álpa-s*, small, cf. lith. *alpnas*, weak.

But we often find skr. *l* = idg. *r* (cf. § 42):

skr. *luñcāmi*, I pull out, I pull off &c., cf. gr. *ὀρύσσω*, lat. *runcāre*.

skr. *lumpámi*, I break, cf. lat. *rumpō*, ags. *réofan*.

Labial explosives.

§ 78. **Skr. p.** Skr. *p* = idg. *p*:

skr. *purás*, in front &c., gr. *πάρος*, cf. goth. *faúra*.

skr. *paraçú-ṣ*, axe, gr. *πέλεκυς*, cf. goth. *filhan*.

skr. *pṛ́çni-ṣ*, speckled, cf. gr. *περκνός* and perhaps ohg. *forhana*.

skr. *parut*, last year, cf. gr. *πέρυσι*, mhg. *vërt*.

skr. *prá-*, forward, gr. *πρό*, goth. *fra-*, cf. lat. *prō(d)*.

skr. *plávāmi*, I float &c., gr. πλέω, cf. lat. *pluit* and ags. *fléotan*.

ved. *nápāt*, descendant, lat. *nepōs*, ohg. *nefo*.

skr. *sárpāmi*, I creep &c., gr. ἕρπω, lat. *serpō*.

§ 79. **Skr. ph.** Skr. *ph* = idg. *ph* (cf. § 46)?

skr. *phéna-s*, foam, cf. oslav. *pěna* and ohg. *feim*.

skr. *phalgu-ṣ*, weak, worthless, useless, cf. gr. φελγύνει· ἀσυνετεῖ, ληρεῖ (Hesych.).

skr. *çaphá-s*, hoof, cf. ohg. *huof*.

§ 80. **Skr. b.** Skr. *b* = idg. *b*:

skr. *bála-m*, strength, power, cf. oslav. *bolij* and lat. *dēbilis*.

skr. *buk-kāra-s*, roar, bellow, cf. gr. βύκτης, βυκάνη, lat. *būcina*.

skr. *lámbate*, hangs down, cf. lat. *lābitur*.

ved. *upa-bdá-s*, stamping, trampling, cf. gr. ἐπίβδαι.

In the neighbourhood of a following aspirate *b* often represents idg. *bh*:

skr. *bódhāmi*, I perceive, goth. *biuda*, cf. gr. πεύθομαι, πυνθάνομαι.

ved. *budhná-s*, bottom, cf. gr. πυθμήν, πύνδαξ, lat. *fundus* and ohg. *bodam*.

In younger texts we often meet with dialectic words, in which *b* is written instead of *v*.

§ 81. **Skr. bh.** Skr. *bh* = idg. *bh*:

skr. *bhárāmi*, I bear, gr. φέρω, lat. *ferō*, goth. *baíra*.

skr. *bhávāmi*, I am, cf. gr. φύω, lat. *fui*, ohg. *būan*.

skr. *bhrū-ṣ*, eye-brow, cf. gr. ὀφρῦς and ohg. *brāwa*.

skr. *nábhas*, cloud, sky, gr. νέφος, cf. νεφέλη, lat. *nebula*, ohg. *nebul*.

skr. *jámbha-s*, set of teeth, tooth, gr. γόμφος, ohg. *chamb*.

Dental explosives.

§ 82. **Skr. t.** Skr. *t* = idg. *t*:
skr. *tanú-ṣ*, thin, gr. ταvυ-, cf. lat. *tenuis*, ohg. *dunni*.
skr. *tudā́mi*, I push, I strike, cf. lat. *tundō* and goth. *stautan*.
skr. *tráyas*, three, gr. τρεῖς, lat. *trēs*, goth. *þreis*.
skr. *pátāmi*, I fly, I fall, lat. *petō*, cf. gr. πέτομαι, πίπτω.
skr. *kártāmi* (more common *kṛntā́mi*), I cut, lith. *kertu*.
skr. *pátnī*, lady, mistress, wife, cf. gr. πότνια.
In the combination *ts* the skr. *t* often goes back on idg. *s*:
skr. *vatsyā́mi*, I shall put on, gr. ἕσσω.
skr. *vidvátsu*, loc. plur. of *vidvā́ṁs-*, knowing.

§ 83. **Skr. th.** Skr. *th* = idg. *th* (cf. § 49):
skr. *véttha*, thou knowest, gr. οἶσθα, cf. goth. *waist*.
In Sanskrit there are very few words beginning with *th*: these few partly have an onomatopoetic character and partly are borrowed from other dialects.

§ 84. **Skr. d.** Skr. *d* = idg. *d*:
skr. *dádāmi*, I give, gr. δίδωμι, cf. lat. *dō*.
skr. *dáça*, ten, gr. δέκα, lat. *decem*, goth. *taíhun*.
skr. *dvā́u*, ved. *dvā́*, two, gr. δύω, lat. *duō*, cf. goth. pl. *twai*.
skr. *ádmi*, I eat, cf. gr. ἔδω, lat. *edō*, goth. *ita*.
skr. *chinádmi*, I cut off, cf. gr. σχίζω, σχινδαλμός, lat. *scindō*.
Before *bh* the skr. *d* sometimes goes back on idg. *z*:
ved. *mādbhíṣ*, instr. pl. of *mā́s*, moon, month.
Skr. *ed* in some cases represents ar. *azd* (see § 63):
ved. *sedyā́t*, 3 pers. sing. optat. perf. of *sad-*, to sit, avest. *hazdyāþ*.

In the neighbourhood of a following aspirate *d* often goes back on idg. *dh*:
skr. *dádhāmi*, I put, gr. τίθημι.

§ 85. **Skr. dh.** Skr. *dh* = idg. *dh*:

skr. *dhárṣāmi*, I dare, cf. gr. θρασύς, θαρρέω, goth. *ga-dars*.

skr. *dhūmá-s*, smoke, vapor, gr. θῦμός, lat. *fūmus*.

skr. *dháyāmi*, I suck, I drink, goth. *daddja*, cf. gr. θῆσθαι, lat. *fēlāre*, *fēmina*.

skr. *mádhu*, honey, gr. μέθυ, ohg. *meto*.

skr. *mádhya-s*, middle, gr. μέσος, lat. *medius*, goth. *midjis*.

In the combinations *bdh*, *ddh*, *gdh* the skr. *dh* often goes back on an original *t*:

ved. *dábdhum*, to hurt: *dabhnómi*, I hurt.

ved. *baddhá-s*, bound: *badhnámi*, I bind.

skr. *dágdhum*, to burn: *dáhāmi*, I burn.

Skr. *edh* sometimes represents ar. *azdh* (see § 63):

skr. *edhí*, imper. of *as-*, to be, cf. avest. *zdī* and gr. ἴσθι.

Lingual explosives.

§ 86. **Skr. ṭ.** Skr. *ṭ* may correspond to idg. *t* (after *ṣ* and in prācritisms), to idg. *lt* and in loans from Prākrit dialects to idg. *rt*.

Skr. *ṭ* (after *ṣ*) = idg. *t*:

skr. *aṣṭáu*, ved. *aṣṭá*, eight, gr. ὀκτώ, lat. *octō*, goth. *ahtau*.

skr. *uṣṭá-s*, burned, lat. *ustus*.

Skr. *ṭ* (in prācritisms) = idg. *t*:

skr. *aṭāmi*, I roam, I wander about, ved. *átāmi*.

skr. *caṭāmi*, I hide myself, ved. *cátāmi*.

Skr. *ṭ* = idg. *lt*:

skr. *paṭa-s*, woven stuff, cloth, garment, cf. oslav. *platĭno*, russ. *polotnó*, linen.

skr. *páṭu-ṣ*, sharp, cf. gr. πλατύς, saltish.

skr. *sphâṭāmi*, I burst, cf. ohg. *spaltan*.

Skr. *ṭ* (in prācritisms) = idg. *rt*:

skr. *bhaṭa-s*, soldier: *bhṛtá-s*, hired (cf. gr. *φέρω*).

skr. *káṭa-s*, mat: *kartana-m*, spinning (cf. gr. *κύρτος*, *κάρταλος*, lat. *crātēs*, goth. *haúrds*).

skr. *kaṭú-ṣ*, sharp: *kart-*, to cut (cf. lith. *kartus*).

The *ṭ* in the nom. sing. and loc. pl. of the stems ending in *ç*, *j*, *ṣ* is to be explained by analogy:

skr. *víṭ*, clan, people, nom. of *viç-*, cf. *veça-s*, house, gr. *οἶκος*, lat. *vīcus* and goth. *weihs*. The regular nominative of *viç-* would have been **vik* (from **vikṣ*, idg. **u̯ik̂-s*).

skr. *rā́ṭ*, king, nom. of *rāj-*, cf. lat. *rēx*, gen. *rēgis*. Here also might have been expected a nominative ending in *k*, viz. **rāk* (from **rākṣ*, idg. **rēk̂-s*).

skr. *dviṭ*, hating, nom. of *dviṣ-*. The regular nominative would have been **dvik* (from **dvikṣ*, idg. **du̯is-s*).

In the *bh*-cases of these stems *ḍ* was regular: *viḍbhíṣ* from idg. **u̯iĝbhis*, *rāḍbhíṣ* from idg. **rēĝbhis*, *dviḍbhíṣ* from idg. **du̯izbhis*, see § 60 and § 63. These cases made it possible, that a locat. pl. and a nom. sing. with *ṭ* were formed.

§ 87. **Skr. ṭh.** Skr. *ṭh* = idg. *lth*:

skr. *jaṭhara-m*, belly, womb, cf. goth. *kilþei*.

skr. *kuṭhāra-s*, axe, lat. *culter*.

In prācritisms *ṭh* sometimes occurs instead of *th*. At the beginning of words *ṭh* is very rare.

§ 88. **Skr. ḍ.** Skr. *ḍ* may represent idg. *ld*, *zd*, *z*, *ĝ* and in prācritisms idg. *d* and *rd*.

Skr. *ḍ* = idg. *ld*:

skr. *jaḍa-s*, cold &c., cf. lat. *gelu*, *gelāre*, icel. *kala* &c. (?).

Skr. *ḍ* = idg. *zd* (after *ĭ*, *ŭ*, *i̯*, *u̯*):

skr. *nīḍá-s*, nest, lat. *nīdus*, ohg. *nest*.

Skr. *ḍ* = idg. *z* (after *ĭ*, *ŭ*, *i̯*, *u̯* before *bh*):

skr. *dviḍbhíṣ*, instr. pl. of *dviṣ-*, hating.

Skr. *ḍ* = idg. *ĝ* (before *bh*):

skr. *viḍbhíṣ*, instr. pl. of *viç-*, clan, people.

§ 89. **Skr. ḍh.** Skr. *ḍh* may represent idg. *ldh*, *zdh*, *ĝh* + *t* and in prācritisms idg. *rdh* and *dh*.

Skr. *ḍh* = idg. *ldh*: no certain example.

Skr. *ḍh* = idg. *zdh* (after *ĭ*, *ŭ*, *i̯*, *u̯*):

ved. *ástoḍhvam*, 2 pers. pl. aor. med. of *stáumi*, I praise.

Skr. *ḍh* = idg. *ĝh* + *t*:

skr. *léḍhi*, licks: *léhmi*, I lick.

skr. *dṛḍhá-s*, firm: *dṛ́hyāmi*, I make firm.

skr. *vóḍhum*, to carry, *váhāmi*, I carry.

Guttural explosives.

§ 90. **Skr. k.** In general skr. *k* represents the idg. *q* and *k*.

Skr. *k* = idg. *q*:

skr. *kā́sate*, coughs, cf. ags. *hwósta*.

skr. *katará-s*, who (from two), gr. πότερος, goth. *hwaþar*.

skr. *yákṛt*, liver, cf. gr. ἧπαρ, lat. *jecur*.

skr. *paṅktí-ṣ*, row of five, row, cf. gr. πέμπτος.

Skr. *k* = idg. *k*:

skr. *kakút* (*d*), summit, cf. lat. *cacūmen*.

skr. *karká-s*, crab, cf. gr. καρκίνος, lat. *cancer*.

ved. *kravíṣ*, raw flesh, gr. κρέας, cf. lat. *cruor*.

The combination *kṣ* may go back on different consonant-groups.

Skr. *kṣ* = idg. *ks* (*qs*):

skr. *dhakṣyā́mi*, I shall burn, lith. *deksiu*, cf. skr. *dáhāmi*, I burn, lith. *degu* (also skr. *ni-dāghá-*, heat, summer, opruss. *dagis*, summer, goth. *dags* &c.).

skr. *vákṣi*, 2 pers. of *vácmi*, I say, cf. *vácas*, word, *vák*, voice, gr. *ἔπος*, *ὀπ-*, lat. *vōx* &c.

skr. *vakṣyámi*, fut. of *vácmi*, I say.

skr. *úkṣāmi*, I grow, perf. *vavákṣa*, cf. gr. *ἀέξω*, goth. *wahsjan* &c. Lith. *auksztas*, high, proves, that we have to do with idg. *ks*.

Skr. *kṣ* = idg. *k̂s*:

skr. *vákṣi*, 2 pers. of *váçmi*, I will, cf. gr. *ἑκών*.

skr. *ákṣa-s*, axle, cf. gr. *ἄξων*, lat. *axis*, ohg. *ahsa*, lith. *aszis*, oslav. *osĭ*.

skr. *dákṣiṇa-s*, right, southern, avest. *dašina-*, oslav. *desĭnŭ*, lith. fem. *deszinė*, cf. gr. *δεξιός*, lat. *dexter*, goth. *taíhswa*.

Skr. *kṣ* = idg. *ss* (after *ĭ*, *ŭ*, *i̯*, *u̯*):

skr. *dvékṣi*, 2 pers. of *dvéṣmi*, I hate.

skr. *çokṣyámi*, I shall dry up, gr. *αὕσω*.

Skr. *kṣ* = guttural + *p* (*đ*): see § 67.

§ 91. **Skr. kh.** Skr. *kh* = idg. *kh* (*qh*):

skr. *çaṅkhá-s*, shell, gr. *κόγχος*.

skr. *skhálāmi*, I stumble, cf. gr. *σφάλλω*?

§ 92. **Skr. g.** Skr. *g* corresponds to idg. *g̑*, *g*.

Skr. *g* = idg. *g̑*:

skr. *gáu-ṣ*, bull, cow, gr. *βοῦς*, lat. **vōs* (*bōs*), ohg. *chuo*.

skr. *gurú-ṣ*, heavy, cf. gr. *βαρύς*, goth. *kaúrus* (also lat. *gravis*).

skr. *ágāt*, went, gr. *ἔβη*.

Skr. *g* = idg. *g*:

skr. *yugá-m*, yoke, age, gr. *ζυγόν*, lat. *jugum*, goth. *juk*.

skr. *ugrá-s*, mighty, terrible, cf. lat. *augeō*, goth. *aukan*.

In the neighbourhood of a following aspirate we often find *g* from *g̑h* or *gh*:

skr. *gṛ́dhyāmi*, I am eager, cf. goth. *grēdus*.

§ 93. **Skr. gh.** Skr. *gh* goes back on idg. *g̑h* or *gh*.

Skr. *gh* = idg. *g̑h*:

skr. *ghaná-s*, slayer (ved.), compact &c., gr. *φόνος*, cf. ohg. *gundea*, ags. *gúđ*.

Skr. *gh* = idg. *gh*:

skr. *dīrghá-s*, long, cf. gr. *δολιχός*.

Palatal affricates.

§ 94. **Skr. c.** Skr. *c* in general represents idg. *q*, *k* before palatal vowels and *i̯*.

Skr. *c* = idg. *q*:

skr. *carú-ṣ*, pot, kettle, icel. *hverr*.

skr. *catvā́ras*, four, goth. *fidwōr*, cf. gr. *τέσσαρες*, lat. *quatuor*.

skr. *pañca*, five, gr. *πέντε*, lat. *quinque*, goth. *fimf*.

Skr. *c* = idg. *k*:

skr. *cyávate*, moves, falls, cf. gr. *σεύω*.

skr. *rócate*, shines, pleases, cf. gr. *λευκός*, lat. *lūx*, *lūcet*, goth. *liuhaþ*.

In cases as *ucca-*, high, the first *c* is an assimilated *t* (here originally *d*).

§ 95. **Skr. ch.** On the origin of skr. *ch* see § 55. Instances:

skr. *chinádmi*, I cut off, cf. avest. *sid-*, gr. *σχίζω*, lat. *scindō*.

skr. *gácchati*, goes, cf. avest. *jasaiti*, gr. *βάσκω*.

§ 96. **Skr. j.** Skr. *j* represents the idg. *g̑*, *g*, before palatal vowels and *i̯*, as well as the idg. *ĝ*.

Skr. *j* = idg. *g̑*:

ved. *járate*, crackles, invokes, cf. ohg. *quirit*.

Skr. *j* = idg. *g*:

skr. *ójas*, strength, power, cf. *ugrá-s*, mighty, terrible, lat. *augeō* and goth. *aukan*.

Skr. *j* = idg. *ĝ*:

ved. *jánas*, race, family, gr. *γένος*, lat. *genus*, cf. goth. *kuni*.

skr. *jā́nu*, knee, cf. gr. *γόνυ*, lat. *genu*, goth. *kniu*.

skr. *juṣā́mi*, I take pleasure, I relish, cf. gr. *γεύω*, goth. *kiusa* and lat. *gustus*, goth. *kustus*.

skr. *bhū́rja-s*, birch, cf. ohg. *pirihha*.

skr. *mṛjā́mi*, I rub, wipe, strip, cf. gr. *ἀμέλγω*, lat. *mulgeō*, ohg. *milchu*.

In cases as ved. *újjiti-ṣ*, victory, the first *j* is an assimilated *d*.

In the neighbourhood of a following aspirate *j* may represent the idg. aspirates *g̯h*, *gh*, *ĝh*:

skr. *jagrā́ha*, seized: *gṛhṇā́mi*.

skr. *jáhāti*, leaves, avest. *zazāiti*.

§ 97. **Skr. jh.** In skr. *ujjhitá-s*, left, from *ud* + **jhitá-s*, the skr. *jh* goes back on idg. *ĝh*: cf. *jáhāmi*, I leave. Most words containing *jh* are not clear.

Spirants.

§ 98. **Skr. ç.** In general skr. *ç* corresponds to idg. *k̂*, but in some cases it is an assimilated *s*.

Skr. *ç* = idg. *k̂*:

skr. *çatá-m*, hundred, gr. *ἑ-κατόν*, lat. *centum*, goth. *hund*.

skr. *çaṅkú-ṣ*, wedge, oslav. *sąkŭ*, branch.

skr. *çáṁsāmi*, I praise, I recite &c., cf. lat. *censeō*.

skr. *veça-s*, house, gr. *οἶκος*, lat. *vīcus*, cf. goth. *weihs*.

skr. *dáçāmi*, I bite, cf. gr. *δάκνω*.

ved. *áçmā* (*n*), stone, gr. *ἄκμων*.

skr. *dadárça*, I have seen, gr. *δέδορκα*.

Skr. *ç* = idg. *s*:

skr. *çváçura-s*, father in law, gr. ἑκυρός, cf. lat. *socer* and goth. *swaíhra*.

skr. *çaçá-s*, hare, cf. ohg. *haso*.

§ 99. **Skr. ṣ.** Skr. *ṣ* lingualized from idg. *s*:

skr. *tíṣṭhāmi*, I stand, gr. ἵστημι.

skr. *uṣṭá-s*, burned, lat. *ustus*.

skr. *vṛ́keṣu*, loc. pl. of *vṛ́ka-s*, wolf, cf. oslav. *vlŭcěchŭ*.

ved. *joṣṭar-*, loving, cf. gr. γευστήριον.

skr. *dvékṣi*, 2 pers. of *dvéṣmi*, I hate.

skr. *dhṛṣṇómi*, *dhárṣāmi*, I dare, cf. gr. θαρρέω and goth. *gadars*.

In the combination *ṣṭ* the skr. *ṣ* often represents idg. *k̂*:

skr. *aṣṭā́* (ved.), *aṣṭā́u*, eight, gr. ὀκτώ, lat. *octō*, goth. *ahtau*.

skr. *diṣṭi-ṣ*, indication &c., cf. ohg. *inziht*, lat. *dictiō*, gr. δεῖξις.

How the *ṣ* of *ṣaṭ*, six, is to be explained, is yet uncertain: probably an initial consonant has been lost, cf. avest. *χšvaš*.

Skr. *ṣ* = idg. *p*, *đ*: see § 67.

§ 100. **Skr. s.** Skr. *s* = idg. *s*:

skr. *saptá*, seven, gr. ἑπτά, lat. *septem*, cf. goth. *sibun*.

ved. *sána-s*, old, gr. fem. ἕνη, cf. lat. *senex* and goth. *sineigs*.

skr. *sáhas*, strength, might, violence, goth. *sigis*.

skr. *svásā* (*r*), sister, lat. *soror*, goth. *swistar*.

skr. *srávāmi*, I flow, I stream, gr. ῥέω, cf. ohg. *stroum*.

skr. *váste*, clothes one's self, puts on, cf. gr. ἕννυμι, ἐσθής, lat. *vestis*, goth. *wasjan*.

§ 101. **Skr. h.** Skr. *h* may go back on idg. *gh*, *gh* before palatal vowels and *i̯*, further on idg. *ĝh* and in dialectic words and forms on idg. *bh* and *dh*.

Skr. *h* = idg. *gh*:

skr. *hánmi*, I slay, cf. gr. θείνω and skr. *hatyā*, slaughter, ohg. *gundea*, ags. *gúđ*.

ved. *háras*, heat, gr. θέρος.

Skr. *h* = idg. *gh*:

ved. *drúhas*, harming spirits, cf. *drúhyāmi*, I harm, ohg. *triogan*.

Skr. *h* = idg. *ĝh*:

ved. *héman-*, winter, gr. χεῖμα, χειμών, cf. gr. χιών, lat. *hiems* &c.

skr. *haṁsá-s*, goose, swan &c., cf. gr. χήν, lat. *anser*, ohg. *gans*.

skr. *bāhú-ṣ*, arm, gr. πῆχυς, ohg. *buog*.

skr. *léhmi*, I lick, cf. gr. λείχω, lat. *lingō*, goth. *-laigōn*.

Skr. *h* = idg. *bh*:

skr. *hárāmi*, I bear, I take, cf. *bhárāmi*, I bear, gr. φέρω &c.

skr. *gṛhṇámi*, I seize, cf. ved. *gṛbhṇámi*.

Skr. *h* = idg. *dh*:

Skr. *-hi*, suffix of the 2 pers. sing. imperat. act., cf. *-dhi*, gr. -θι.

skr. *-mahe*, *-mahi*, suffixes of the 1 pers. pl. med., gr. -μεθα.

In some words the skr. *h* seems to correspond to gr. γ, goth. *k*: see § 66.

PART III.

SANDHI-SYSTEM.

§ 102. **General remarks.** The rules, which govern the changes of the initial and final sounds of words in the sentence and in composition, are called *sandhi*-rules. Of course already in the mother-language the final sounds of preceding words and the initial sounds of following words had a mutual influence on each other, but it is impossible to reconstruct a complete tableau of this Indogermanic sandhi. Yet there are reasons to suppose, that already in the Indogermanic period the explosives and spirants were voiced or voiceless according to their position before voiced or voiceless explosives and spirants. The double forms gr. *προτί* = skr. *práti* and gr. *πρός* = skr. *práty* may prove, that in the mother-language *i* before sonants became a semivowel, which suggests the supposition, that this was also the case with *u*. The simultaneous existence of the Indian dual-endings *-āu* = goth. *-au* (in *ahtau*) and *-ā* = gr. *-ω* allows the conclusion, that yet in a time of dialectic continuity the idg. diphthong *-ōu̯* before certain consonants or groups of consonants was simplified to *-ō*. Gr. *ἄκμων* and skr. *áçmā*, gr. *πατήρ* and skr. *pitā́* stand in a similar relation to each other. By the side of roots beginning with *s* we often find doublets without that initial consonant (skr. *sthágāmi*: lat. *tegō*, goth. *stautan*: skr. *tudā́mi*) and hence we may conclude, that before the end of the Indogermanic period the initial *s* was lost, when preceded by a word ending in *s*. About these and other phenomena, which are explained by Indogermanic sandhi, see Brugmann 1, 490 sqq.

The Indian sandhi has gradually developed itself from that of the mother-language, because of which only a historical treatment of the sandhi-rules may claim a scientific value, but the uncertainty, which till now prevails in the history of the initial and final sounds, makes it preferable to arrange them systematically.

§ 103. **Final and initial vowels.** It is a rule in composition as well as in the sentence, that *-ă* + *ă-* are contracted to *ā*, *-ĭ* + *ĭ-* to *ī*, *-ŭ* + *ŭ-* to *ū*. An *a*-vowel (*-ă*) combines with an *i*-vowel (*ĭ-*) to *e*, with an *u*-vowel (*ŭ-*) to *o*, with *ṛ-* to *ar*, with *e-* and *āi-* to *āi*, with *o-* and *āu-* to *āu*, but *-ĭ*, *-ŭ* and *-ṛ* before a dissimilar vowel or diphthong are changed each to its corresponding consonant (*y*, *v*, *r*). The original, but contracted diphthongs *-e* and *-o* remain unchanged before *a-*, which however disappears; before all other vowels they become *a* (we seldom find *-ay* and *-av*, which of course are the regular representatives of the antevocalic ar. *-ai̯* and *-au̯*: see § 7). The diphthongs *-āi* and *-āu* before all vowels may be retained unchanged (if so, they are written *-āy*, *-āv*), but it is also permitted to change them to *-ā*.

About some liberty in Sanskrit as to the treatment of final and initial vowels see Whitney § 127 *a*, § 129 *c*, § 133 *a*, § 134 *c* and cf. Kern, Taal en letteren 6, 332. The peculiarities of the Vedic vowelsandhi are noticed in Whitney's grammar, to which it will suffice to refer.

Contraction of similar vowels:

na + *asti* = *nāsti*, not is.

tatra + *āyātaḥ* = *tatrāyātaḥ*, there arrived.

gatvā + *abravīt* = *gatvābravīt*, having gone he (she) said.

rājā + *ādadāt* = *rājādadāt*, the king took.

asti + *iha* = *astīha*, is here.

adhi + *īçvaraḥ* = *adhīçvaraḥ*, over-lord.

devī + *iyam* = *devīyam*, this goddess.

strī + *īkṣate* = *strīkṣate*, the woman sees.

su + *uktam* = *sūktam*, hymn.

bāhu- + *ūru-* = *bāhūru-*, arms and thighs.

Combination of *ă* with dissimilar vowels:

tiṣṭha + *iha* = *tiṣṭheha*, remain here.

ratha- + *īṣā* = *ratheṣā*, shaft of a chariot.

bhāryā + *iva* = *bhāryeva*, as a wife.

kā + *īdṛçī* = *kedṛçī*, who (fem.) is such a one.

huta- + *ucchiṣṭam* = *hutocchiṣṭam*, remains of a sacrifice.

vṛka- + *udara-* = *vṛkodara-*, who has a wolf's belly (epithet of Bhīma).

sahasā + *utthāya* = *sahasotthāya*, hastily arisen.

rambhā- + *ūru-* = *rambhoru-*, who has thighs as a banana.

sapta + *ṛṣayaḥ* = *saptarṣayaḥ*, the seven sages, the seven stars of the Great Bear.

mahā- + *ṛṣabhaḥ* = *maharṣabhaḥ*, a great (large) bull.

eka- + *ekaḥ* = *ekāikaḥ*, each.

mā + *evam* = *māivam*, not so (prohibitively).

jala- + *okas-* = *jalāukas-*, whose dwelling-place is the water, aquatic animal, leech.

mahā- + *oṣadhiḥ* = *mahāuṣadhiḥ*, a great simple.

loka- + *āiçvaryam* = *lokāiçvaryam*, dominion of the world.

mahā- + *āiçvaryam* = *mahāiçvaryam*, great dominion.

rūpa- + *āudārya-* = *rūpāudārya-*, beauty and generosity.

yathā + *āucityam* = *yathāucityam*, properly (according to custom).

Change of *ĭ*, *ŭ*, *ṛ* to *y*, *v*, *r* before dissimilar vowels:

iti + *uktvā* = *ityuktvā*, having spoken thus.

kuṭṭanī + *āha* = *kuṭṭanyāha*, the procuress said.

madhu + *iva* = *madhviva*, as honey.

pitṛ- + *artham* = *pitrartham*, for the father's sake.

Treatment of *e* and *o* before vowels:

tathāgate + *api* = *tathāgate'pi*, even under such circumstances, nevertheless.

bhāno + *atra* = *bhāno'tra*, sun (vocat.), here.

te + *āgatāḥ* = *ta āgatāḥ*, they have arrived.

nagare + *iha* = *nagara iha*, here in the town.

sūno + *ehi* = *sūna(v) ehi*, son (vocat.), come.

Treatment of *āi*, *āu* before vowels:

tasmāi + *adadāt* = *tasmā(y) adadāt*, he (she) gave him.

tāu + *ūcatuḥ* = *tā(v) ūcatuḥ*, those two said.

Certain final vowels maintain themselves unchanged before any following vowel (Whitney § 138):

1° the vowels *ī*, *ū* and *e* as dual endings, both in nominal and in verbal forms;

2° the pronoun *amī* (nom. pl.), those;

3° the vowels of interjections as *aho*, *he* &c.

Some other exceptions to the vowel-sandhi are of less importance.

§ 104. **Simplification of consonant-groups.** The final *s* (*ṣ*) and *t* disappeared, when preceded by one or more consonants. If there remained after the dropping of *s* (*ṣ*) or *t* an other combination than *r* + explosive, even that was simplified. About probable traces of postconsonantic *t* and *s* see § 105.

Dropping of postconsonantic *s* (*ṣ*):

vāk from **vāk-ṣ*, voice, cf. avest. *vāχš*, lat. *vōx*.

adhok from **adhok-ṣ*, 2 pers. sing. impf. of *dohmi*, I milk.

pāt from **pāt-s*, foot, cf. gr. dor. πώς.

açāt from **açāt-s*, older **açās-s*, 2 pers. sing. impf. of *çāsmi*, I rule &c.: see § 62. The form *açāt* as 2 pers. does not seem to occur in literature, but is warranted by its *ts* from *ss*. The 3 pers. is also *açāt*, but here the *t* is not regular: **açās-t* would have given **açās*. It is not surprising, that the organic paradigm *açāsam*, *açāt*, *açās* has been changed by analogy to *açāsam*, *açās*, *açāt*.

ajāiṣ (*ajāiḥ*, see § 109) from **ajāiṣt*, 3 pers. sing. aor. of *jayāmi*, I conquer.

ahan from **ahan-s*, 2 pers. sing. impf. of *hanmi*, I slay.

vṛkān, *agnīn*, *paraçūn* from **vṛkāns*, **agnīns*, **paraçūns*, acc. pl. of *vṛka-s*, wolf, *agni-ṣ*, fire, *paraçu-ṣ*, axe, cf. goth. *dagans*, *anstins*, *sununs*, gr. cret. λύκονς, τρίνς, υἱύνς &c.

akar from **akar-ṣ*, 2 pers. sing. aor. of *karomi*, I make.

Dropping of postconsonantic *t*:

adhok from **adhok-t*, 3 pers. sing. impf. of *dohmi*, I milk.

ahan from **ahan-t*, 3 pers. sing. impf. of *hanmi*, I slay.

akar from **akar-t*, 3 pers. sing. aor. of *karomi*, I make.

Dropping of two or more consonants:

prāṅ from **prāṅk-ṣ*, eastern.

bharan from **bharant-s*, bearing, cf. goth. *baírands*.

achān from **achānts-t*, 3 pers. sing. aor. (1 pers. *achāntsam*) of *chand-*, to appear, to please.

Examples of *r* + explosive remaining unchanged after the loss of a final *s* (*ṣ*):

ūrk from **ūrk-ṣ*, strength, vigor.

suhārt from **suhārt-s*, having a good heart.

In cases as *viṭ*, *dviṭ* &c. the *ṭ* is not organic: see § 86.

§ 105. **Final nasals.** In general it is a rule, that final nasals, as to the place of their articulation, are assimilated to a following consonant, but before labials and gutturals *-n* is not modified.

The *-n*, *-ñ* (from *-n*), *-ṇ* (from *-n*) before a following *t-* (*th-*), *c-* (*ch-*), *ṭ* (*ṭh-*) usually insert a sibilant: its mode of articulation depends on the following initial consonant. Before the inserted sibilant the nasal becomes anusvāra. The origin of this rule is probably due to the circumstance, that the idg. *-ns* was simplified to *-n* (see § 104), except before those voiceless dentals, palatal affricates and linguals.

The combination of *-n* + *ç-* is *-ñ ç-* as well as *-ñ ch-*. In the same way *-n* + *s-* and *-n* + *ṣ-* are often combined to *-nt s-*, *-nt ṣ-*.

The *-n* before *l-* is assimilated to *-l*, after nasalizing the preceding vowel. The labial nasal *-m* before *y-*, *v-*, *r-*, *l-*, *h-* and sibilants becomes anusvāra.

All nasals except *-m*, when preceded by a short vowel, are doubled before any initial vowel.

Partial assimilation of nasals to initial consonants:

tam + *daridram* = *tan daridram*, that poor man (acc.).
apaçyam + *ḍākinim* = *apaçyaṇ ḍākinim*, I saw a witch.
imam + *kumāram* = *imaṅ kumāram*, this boy (acc.)
pāṇim + *jagrāha* = *pāṇiñ jagrāha*, I (he) seized the hand.
pakṣin + *ḍayase* = *pakṣiṇ ḍayase*, bird (voc.), thou art flying.
tān + *janān* = *tāñ janān*, those people (acc.).

Examples of *-n* before voiceless dentals, palatal affricates and linguals:

tān + *tarūn* = *tāṁs tarūn*, those trees (acc.).
tān + *cārān* = *tāṁç cārān*, those spies (acc.).

tān + *ṭaṅkān* = *tāṁṣ ṭaṅkān*, those pickaxes (acc.)

In many cases this *s* (*ç*, *ṣ*) has an etymological value: *tān* goes back on idg. **tons* (gr. cret. *τόνς*, goth. *þans*) and so *tāṁs tarūn* regularly represents an original **tons teruns*.

Examples of *-n* before sibilants:

tān + *çatrūn* = *tāñ çatrūn* or *tāñ chatrūn*, those enemies (acc.).

mahān + *san* = *mahān san* or *mahānt san*, being great.

tān + *ṣaṭ* = *tān ṣaṭ* or *tānt ṣaṭ*, those six (acc.)

Example of *-n* + *l-*:

tān + *lokān* = *tāṁl lokān*, those worlds (acc.).

Examples of *-m* before semivowels, liquids, *h-* and sibilants:

tām + *yātrām* = *tāṁ yātrām*, that festive train (acc.).

gahanam + *vanam* = *gahanaṁ vanam*, a thick forest.

bahumūlyam + *ratnam* = *bahumūlyaṁ ratnam*, a precious jewel.

tam + *laguḍam* = *taṁ laguḍam*, that cudgel (acc.).

vṛkam + *hanmi* = *vṛkaṁ hanmi*, I slay a wolf.

jalam + *sravati* = *jalaṁ sravati*, the water flows.

vīrāṇām + *çāuryam* = *vīrāṇāṁ çāuryam*, the valor of heroes.

çoṇitam + *ṣṭhīvati* = *çoṇitaṁ ṣṭhīvati*, he (she) spits blood.

Gemination of nasals after a short vowel:

gacchan + *apatat* = *gacchann apatat*, going, he fell.

pratyaṅ + *āsīnaḥ* = *pratyaṅṅ āsīnaḥ*, sitting towards the west.

But:

annam + *icchati* = *annam icchati*, he (she) desires food.

§ 106. **Voiced and voiceless explosives.** In general Sanskrit has maintained the Indogermanic rules. Voiced explosives become voiceless before voiceless consonants and in pausa; voiceless explosives become voiced before voiced consonants and (a specific Sanskrit phenomenon) before vowels. The change of tenues to mediae before vowels is to be explained by analogy: see Brugmann 1, 494.

Change of mediae to tenues before voiceless consonants and in pausa:

tad + *phalam* = *tat phalam*, that fruit.

tasmād + *samudrād* = *tasmāt samudrāt*, from that ocean.

Change of tenues to mediae before voiced consonants and vowels:

ṛtvik + *bhāṣate* = *ṛtvig bhāṣate*, the priest speaks.

avasat + *vārāṇasyām* = *avasad vārāṇasyām*, he (she) dwelt in Benares.

akrīṇāt + *annam* = *akrīṇād annam*, he (she) bought food.

§ 107. **Explosives before nasals.** Final explosives, when followed by an initial nasal, are converted to their homorganic nasals. Only the assimilation of *-d* to *-n* is in harmony with the general phonetic rules of Sanskrit (see § 50).

Examples:

vāk + *mama* = *vāṅ mama*, my voice.

viḍ- + *mūtra-* = *viṇmūtra-*, faeces and urine (the *ṇ* is to be explained by assuming, that from the *bh-* cases of *viṣ-* a stem *viḍ-* was abstracted, which afterwards was composed with *mūtra-*. The nom. *viṭ* is a similar analogous formation).

tad + *nagaram* = *tan nagaram*, that town.

§ 108. **Assimilation of dental explosives to palatal affricates, to ç, to linguals and to l.** The dental explosives are totally assimilated to the initial consonant of the following word, if this consonant is a nasal (see § 107), a palatal affricate, a lingual or a *l*. With an initial *ç-* the dental explosives are combined to *cch*.

Examples:

tad + *ca* = *tac ca*, and that.

bhavat- + *jāmātā* = *bhavajjāmātā*, your son in law.

atāḍayat + *ḍiṇḍimam* = *atāḍayaḍ ḍiṇḍimam*, he beat the drum.

tad + *loham* = *tal loham*, that iron.

tad + *çṛṇomi* = *tac chṛṇomi*, I hear that.

§ 109. **Treatment of -s and -ṣ.** Only after the Aryan *a* and *ā* the *-s* was preserved unchanged, after *ĭ*, *ŭ* and diphthongs it had become *-ś* before the end of the Aryan period. In Indian this *-ś* was lingualized (*-ṣ*). About *-s* (*-ṣ*) after consonants see § 104. The sandhi-rules concerning *-s* and *-ṣ* may be formulated as follows:

Before *t-* (*th-*) the original *-s* remains unchanged, but *-ṣ* is converted to *-s*; before *ṭ-* (*ṭh-*) the *-ṣ* remains unchanged, but *-s* becomes *-ṣ*; before *c-* (*ch-*) the dental and the lingual sibilants are both palatalized, i. e. converted to *-ç*. As to the conversion of *-ṣ* to *-s* before dentals (*t-*, *th-*) it is to be remarked, that in the Veda often occur cases as *agníṣ ṭvā*, *çúciṣ ṭvám*, in which the assimilation has followed an opposite direction: here the final *-ṣ* has assimilated the initial dental (*agníṣ*, fire, + *tvā*, thee; *çúciṣ*, clear, pure, + *tvám*, thou), which is in harmony with the treatment of *ṣ* + *t* in internal combination (see § 49). Before *k* (*kh*), *p* (*ph*) and in pausa *-s* and *-ṣ* become visarga: yet in the Veda cases as *vā́stoṣ pátiḥ*, *ā́yuṣ kṛṇotu* are not rare (*vā́stoṣ*, gen. of *vā́stu-*, house, + *pátiḥ*, lord; *ā́yuṣ*, long life, + *kṛṇotu*, may he make). Before sibilants *-s* and *-ṣ* are either assimilated or converted to visarga. Before voiced consonants, except *r-*, and before vowels *-ṣ* becomes *-r*, but before *r-* the *-ṣ* disappears after lengthening a preceding *i* or *u*. Before voiced consonants and before *a-* the very common ending *-as* becomes *-o*, but before other vowels it becomes *-a*; in *-ās* the *-s* is dropped before voiced consonants as well as before vowels without leaving any trace. After the *-o*, which goes back on *-as*, an initial *a-* disappears. On the probable course of development of this system see Brugmann 1, 495.

The unchanged *-s* before *t-*:

nṛpas + *tuṣyati* = *nṛpas tuṣyati*, the king is satisfied (pleased).

namas tasmāi = *namas tasmāi*, reverence to him.

Dentalization of *-ṣ* before *t-*:

agniṣ + *tiṣṭhati* = *agnis tiṣṭhati*, a fire stands.

guruṣ + *tāḍayati* = *gurus tāḍayati*, the teacher beats.

The unchanged *-ṣ* before *ṭ-*:

paraçuṣ + *ṭaṅkaç ca* = *paraçuṣ ṭaṅkaç ca*, hatchet and pickaxe.

Lingualization of *-s* before *ṭ-*:

ṭiṭṭibhas + *ṭiṭṭibhī ca* = *ṭiṭṭibhaṣ ṭiṭṭibhī ca*, male and female of Parra jacana.

Palatalization of *-s* and *-ṣ* before *c-* (*ch-*):

kumbhilas + *corayati* = *kumbhilaç corayati*, the thief steals.

çatruṣ + *chinatti* = *çatruç chinatti*, the foe cuts off.

Change of *-s* and *-ṣ* to visarga before *k-*, *kh-*, *p-*, *ph-*:

amātyas + *kupyati* = *amātyaḥ kupyati*, the minister is angry.

taruṣ + *kampate* = *taruḥ kampate*, the tree is trembling, being shaken.

naras + *khādati* = *naraḥ khādati*, the man eats.

paçuṣ + *khidyate* = *paçuḥ khidyate*, the animal is being teased.

khecarās + *patanti* = *khecarāḥ patanti*, the birds fly.

mṛtyoṣ + *pāças* = *mṛtyoḥ pāçaḥ*, the bond of death.

apaçyas + *phalāni* = *apaçyaḥ phalāni*, thou sawest fruits.

Change of *-s* and *-ṣ* to visarga in pausa:

yudhyante + *kṣatriyās* = *yudhyante kṣatriyāḥ*, the noblemen fight.

rakṣati + *nṛpas* = *rakṣati nṛpaḥ*, the king protects.

çūdrāṇām + *jātiṣ* = *çūdrānāñ* (*çūdrāṇāṁ*) *jātiḥ*, the caste of the Çūdra's.

tarati + *nāuṣ* = *tarati nāuḥ*, the ship crosses.

Treatment of *-s* and *-ṣ* before sibilants:

nṛpas + *sīdati* = *nṛpaḥ sīdati* or *nṛpas sīdati*, the king sits.

cakṣuṣ + *sphurati* = *cakṣuḥ sphurati* or *cakṣus sphurati*, the eye twitches.

bālas + *çete* = *bālaḥ çete* or *bālaç çete*, the boy is lying (on a couch &c.).

khadyotās + *ṣaṭpadāç ca* = *khadyotāḥ ṣaṭpadāç ca* or *khadyotāṣ ṣaṭpadāç ca*, fire-flies and bees.

Change of *-ṣ* to *-r* before voiced consonants:

agniṣ + *dahati* = *agnir dahati*, the fire burns.

sādhuṣ + *yacchati* = *sādhur yacchati*, the good man gives.

nāuṣ + *badhyate* = *nāur badhyate*, the ship is being bound.

Change of *-ṣ* to *-r* before vowels:

ṛṣiṣ + *uvāca* = *ṛṣir uvāca*, the sage said.

viṣṇuṣ + *iva* = *viṣṇur iva*, as Vishnu.

gireṣ + *upatyakā* = *girer upatyakā*, the land lying at the foot of the mountain.

gāuṣ + *iyam* = *gāur iyam*, this cow.

Change of *-iṣ* and *-uṣ* to *-ī* and *-ū* before *r-*:

dāçarathiṣ + *rāmas* = *dāçarathī rāmaḥ*, Rāma, the son of Daçaratha.

çiçuṣ + *roditi* = *çiçū roditi*, the child weeps.

Change of *-as* to *-o* before voiced consonants:

açvas + *dhāvati* = *açvo dhāvati*, the horse runs.

mṛgas + *mriyate* = *mṛgo mriyate*, the antilope dies.

Change of *-as* to *-o* before *a-*:

tuṣṭas + *aham* = *tuṣṭo'ham*, I am satisfied (pleased).

yas + *anṛtaṁ vadati* = *yo'nṛtaṁ vadati*, who speaks untruth.

Change of *-as* to *-a* before other vowels than *a-*:

kāulikas + *āha* = *kāulika āha*, the weaver said.

lomaças + *uvāca* = *lomaça uvāca*, Lomaça said.

Change of *-ās* to *-ā* before voiced consonants and before vowels:

vihagās + *ḍayante* = *vihagā ḍayante*, the birds fly.

narās + *vadanti* = *narā vadanti*, the men say.

bālās + *annam pṛcchanti* = *bālā annam pṛcchanti*, the children ask food.

In particular we must notice the treatment of the pronouns *sa*, that, and *eṣa*, this. Though originally they do not end in *-s*, yet their pausa-form is *saḥ*, *eṣaḥ* and before *a-* they appear as *so*, *eṣo*, after the *-o* of which forms the initial *a-* disappears.

Examples:

sa + *dadarça* = *sa dadarça*, he saw.

sa + *pumān* = *sa pumān*, that man.

sa + *avadat* = *so'vadat*, he said.

mūrkhas + *sa* = *mūrkhaḥ saḥ*, he is a fool.

The exclamation *bhoṣ* before vowels and before voiced consonants appears as *bho* (instead of **bhor*): the cause of this irregularity is the origin of the word, which is a contracted form of *bhavas*, voc. of *bhavant-*, your honor (pron. pers. used in reverent allocution).

§ 110. **Treatment of -r.** The sandhi-rules concerning *-r* are but partly the organic result of phonetic processes: much in the sandhi of *-r* is due to analogy. I shall simply give an account of the rules without trying to trace them to their origin.

Before *c-* (*ch-*) the *-r* is turned into *-ç*; before *ṭ-* (*ṭh-*) into *-ṣ*; before *t-* (*th-*) into *-s*. Before *k* (*kh*), *p* (*ph*), before sibilants and in pausa the *-r* becomes visarga. Before an initial *r-* the final *-r* disappears after lengthening a preceding short vowel. In any other case *-r* remains unchanged.

Substitution of sibilants for *r* before *c-* (*ch-*), *ṭ-*, *t-*:

punar + *cacāra* = *punaç cacāra*, again he wandered.

niṣedur + *chāyāyām* = *niṣeduç chāyāyām*, they sat down in the shadow.

pitur + *ṭaṅkas* = *pituṣ ṭaṅkaḥ*, the father's pickaxe.

ūcur + *te* = *ūcus te*, they said.

Change of *-r* to visarga before *k* (*kh*), *p* (*ph*), sibilants and in pausa (only in pausa the change seems to have been organic, see Brugmann 1, 494):

punar + *karoti* = *punaḥ karoti*, again he (she) does.

dadur + *phalāni* = *daduḥ phalāni*, they have given fruits.

babhūvur + *samāje* = *babhūvuḥ samāje*, they were at the assembly.

vanam + *vicerur* = *vanaṁ viceruḥ*, they wandered through the forest.

Change of *-ur*, *-ar* to *-ū*, *-ā* before *r-*:

ūcur + *rāmam* = *ūcū rāmam*, they said to Rāma.

punar + *rakṣati* = *punā rakṣati*, again he protects.

The unchanged *-r* before voiced consonants and before vowels:

pitar + *dehi* = *pitar dehi*, father (voc.), give.

punar + *jagāma* = *punar jagāma*, again he went.

punar + *āha* = *punar āha*, again he said.

dadur + *annam* = *dadur annam*, they gave food.

§ 111. **Changes of initial consonants.** In § 108 we saw, that *ç-* with a preceding dental combines to *cch*. An initial *ch-* becomes *cch-*, when preceded by a short vowel, the preposition (prefix) *ā* or the prohibitive adverb *mā*. Finally we mention the rule, that an initial *h-* is changed to the aspirate of a preceding media, whether this media is original or a softened tenuis (see § 106).

Change of *ch-* to *cch-*:

āhara + *chattram* = *āhara cchattram*, bring the parasol.
ā + *chāditas* = *ācchāditaḥ*, covered.

Change of *h*- to the aspirate of a preceding media:

pṛthak + *haranti* = *pṛthag gharanti*, they take separately.
tad + *hastas* = *taddhastaḥ*, his hand.

PART IV.

ACCENT.

§ 112. **The accent of the Indogermanic period.** Verner's law (Kuhn's Zeitschr. 23, 97 sqq.) has been an evident proof of the fact, that the Indian stress, as it is handed down to us in some Vedic books and by ancient Indian grammarians, generally fell on the same syllables as in the Indogermanic mother-language. In Indian, Balto-Slavonic and Ur-Germanic the so-called *free* accent prevailed, i. e. that neither by the number of syllables nor by the quantity of any syllable the stress was bound to a certain place. Therefore we must assume, that the accent of the mother-language was also a free one. Concerning the accent of the sentence we may learn from the comparison of the Indogermanic languages, that already in a period of dialectic continuity some conjunctions, the interrogative pronouns, when used as indefinites, the personal pronouns, when not used emphatically or antithetically, in many cases also the vocatives and the verbum finitum in an independent clause were deprived of their stress by the preceding word.

Long before the separation of the Indogermanic dialects

all vowels of so-called toneless syllables were weakened: Strachan (Bezz. Beitr. 14, 173 sqq.) and Kretschmer (Kuhn's Zeitschr. 31, 325 sqq.) have shown, that this rule is not to be restricted to pretonic vowels. Many scholars therefore assume, that the Indogermanic accent of an early period must have been a strong expiratorical one (but cf. Finck, Ueber das verhältnis des baltisch-slavischen nominalaccents zum urindogermanischen, Marburg 1895, 29 sqq.) and that it became less expiratorical or even musical towards the end of the proethnic period.

Now there is no longer any doubt, but that the mother-language had two accents of different quality, one of which is represented by the Sanskrit udātta and the Greek *ὀξεῖα*, while the other has left its traces in the dissyllabic value of some long vowels in the Vedic dialect, the Greek *περισπωμένη* and the Lithuanian *schleifton*. See Bezzenberger, Bezz. Beitr. 7, 66 sqq.; Hanssen, Kuhn's Zeitschr. 27, 612 sqq.; Hirt, Idg. forschungen 1, 1 sqq. 195 sqq.

To Hirt we owe an excellent monography on all questions concerning the Indogermanic accentuation (Hirt, Der indogermanische akzent, Strassburg 1895).

§ 113. **Accentual agreement between Sanskrit and Greek.** The liberty of accent, which prevailed in the mother-language, was restricted in Greek by many special rules (see Hirt, Der idg. akzent 24 sqq.). Yet there are many words — dissyllabic and trisyllabic —, which have the same accent in Indian and in Greek.

A few examples will suffice:

skr. *padás*, gr. *ποδός*, gen. of skr. *pát*, foot, gr. dor. *πώς*.
skr. *tráyas*, three, gr. *τρεῖς*, but loc. skr. *triṣú*, cf. gr. *τρισί*.
skr. *páñca*, five, gr. *πέντε*, goth. *fimf*.

skr. *dáça*, ten, gr. δέκα, goth. *taíhun*.
skr. *saptá*, seven, gr. ἑπτά.
skr. *aṣṭā́(u)*, eight, gr. ὀκτώ.
skr. *ṛ́kṣa-s*, bear, gr. ἄρκτος.
skr. *jámbha-s*, set of teeth, gr. γόμφος.
ved. *dáma-s*, house, gr. δόμος.
skr. *áçva-s*, horse, gr. ἵππος, goth. *aíhwa-*.
skr. *ūrdhvá-s*, high, cf. gr. ὀρθός.
ved. *mīḍhá-(m)*, prize, contest, gr. μισθό-(ς).
skr. *dhūmá-s*, smoke, gr. θῡμός.
skr. *yajñá-s*, sacrifice, gr. ἁγνός.
skr. *çrutá-s*, heard, heard of, gr. κλυτός.
skr. *jñātá-s*, known, gr. γνωτός.
skr. *gurú-ṣ*, heavy, gr. βαρύς.
skr. *svādú-ṣ*, sweet, gr. ἡδύς.
skr. *mádhu*, honey, gr. μέθυ.
skr. *nábhas*, sky, gr. νέφος.
ved. *jánas*, race, gr. γένος.
skr. *mánas*, mind, gr. μένος.
skr. *ándhas*, herb, gr. ἄνθος.
skr. *çrávas*, fame, gr. κλέος.
skr. *sádas*, seat, gr. ἕδος.
ved. *bhárma (n)*, bearing, gr. φέρμα.
ved. *hóma (n)*, pouring, oblation, gr. χεῦμα.
ved. *vásma (n)*, cover, gr. lesb. ϝέμμα.
skr. *pitā́*, father, gr. πατήρ, goth. *fadar*.
skr. *devā́*, brother in law, gr. δᾱήρ.
skr. *bhrā́tā*, brother, gr. φρᾱ́τωρ, goth. *brōþar*.
skr. *svásā*, sister, cf. gr. ἔορες.
In trisyllabic words and forms:
skr. *úttara-s*, further, left &c., gr. ὕστερος.

skr. *dúhitar*, gr. *θύγατερ*, voc. of skr. *duhitā́*. daughter, gr. *θυγάτηρ*.

skr. *svā́dīyas* neutr., sweeter, gr. *ἥδιον*.

ved. *aṣṭā́pāt*, with eight feet or parts, gr. *ὀκτώπους*.

skr. *pitáras*, fathers, gr. *πατέρες*.

skr. *janitā́*, father, gr. *γενετήρ*.

ved. *iṣirá-s*, strong, quick &c., gr. *ἱερός*.

skr. *bahulá-s*, numerous &c., gr. *παχυλός*.

§ 114. **Accentual agreement between Sanskrit and Germanic.** It may be useful to give some examples of Verner's law, which agree with the accent of the identical Sanskrit words and forms:

skr. *pitā́*, father, goth. *fadar*, germ. **fađér* from **fapér*.

skr. *ātmā́* (*n*), breath, soul, os. *āđom*, ohg. *ātum*, germ. **ēđmén-* from **ēpmén-*.

skr. *ketú-ṣ*, brightness, light, beam, banner, goth. *haidus*, germ. **χaiđú-s* from **χaipú-s*.

skr. *nakhára-s* (*nakhará-s*), nail, claw, ohg. *nagal*, germ. **nayló-s* from **naχló-s*.

skr. *vṛkī́*, she-wolf, icel. *ylgr*, germ. **ulyu̯í-s* from **ulχu̯í-s*.

skr. *snuṣā́*, daughter in law, ohg. *snura*, germ. **snuzā́* from **snusā́*.

skr. *māṁsá-m*, flesh, meat, goth. *mimz*, germ. **mimzó-m* from **mimsó-m* (**mēṁsó-m*).

In the verbal system:

skr. *svāpáyāmi*, I cause to sleep, cf. ohg. *int-swebbiu*: skr. *svápna-s*, icel. *svefn*.

skr. *vavṛtimá*, 1 pers. pl. perf., *vavṛtāná-*, part. perf. med. of the root *vart-*, to turn &c., ags. *wurdon*, *worden*, ohg. *wurtum*, *giwortan*: skr. *vártana-m*, vb. noun, *vavárta*, 1. 3. pers. sing. perf., ags. *weorđan*, *wearđ*, ohg. *werdan*, *ward*.

skr. *didiçimá*, 1 pers. pl. perf., *didiçānā́-*, part. perf. med. of the root *deç-*, to indicate &c., ags. *tigon, tigen*, ohg. *zigum, gizigan*: skr. *déçana-m*, vb. noun, *didéça*, 1. 3. pers. sing. perf., ags. *téon*, *táh*, ohg. *zīhan*, *zēh*.

skr. *jujuṣimá*, 1 pers. pl. perf., *jujuṣāṇā́-*, part. perf. med., *juṣāṇā́-*, part. aor. med. of the root *joṣ-*, to enjoy, ags. *curon, coren*, ohg. *kurum*, *gikoran*: skr. *jóṣaṇa-m*, vb. noun, *jujóṣa*, 1. 3. pers. sing. perf., ags. *céosan*, *céas*, ohg. *kiosan*, *kōs*.

§ 115. **Dissyllabic value of long vowels.** Dissyllabic value of long vowels in Vedic, corresponding to the Greek *περισπωμένη* and the Lithuanian *schleifton*:

a. Gen. pl., ending in *-ām* (*-aam*), for instance ved. *vṛ́kām* (*vṛ́kaam*), cf. gr. *θεῶν*, lith. *vilkũ*, ohg. *wolfo* (goth. *wulfē*).

b. Abl. sing. of *-a-* stems, ending in *-ad* (*-aad*), for instance *vṛ́kād* (*vṛ́kaad*), cf. lith. *vilkõ*, goth. adv. *þaþrō*.

c. Nom. acc. pl. of *-ā-* stems, ending in *-ās* (*-aas*), for instance *áçvās* (*áçvaas*), cf. lith. nom. pl. *mérgôs* and goth. *gibōs*.

d. Nom. pl. of *-a-* stems, ending in *-ās* (*-aas*). This form is not preserved in Greek and Lithuanian. With *vṛ́kās* (*vṛ́kaas*) only goth. *wulfōs* may be compared.

There are yet other cases, where long vowels of the Vedic dialect have (resp. may have) the metrical value of two syllables, but here it is of no use to cite them all: it will suffice to refer to Hirt, Idg. forschungen 1, 5 sqq.

§ 116. **Accentuation of texts.** The accentuation is marked only in manuscripts of the Saṁhitā's and some other works belonging to the Veda.

The Indian grammarians distinguish the following accents:

1. *udātta-*, i. e. raised, corresponding to the Greek *ὀξεῖα*.
2. *anudātta-*, i. e. not raised, corresponding to the Greek *βαρεῖα*.
3. *svarita-*, see Böhtlingk & Roth. The svarita is nearly

always found on syllables, in which a vowel, be it short or long, is preceded by a *y* or *v* representing an original *i* or *u* with udātta-accent. But there is also a *dependent svarita-*, which falls on all syllables immediately preceded by an udātta, whether in the same or in another word, unless it be followed by a syllable, which bears an udātta or a svarita.

In the hymns of the Ṛgveda the accent is written as follows:

1. The udātta is not marked.

2. The svarita, independent or dependent, is marked by a short perpendicular stroke above.

3. The anudātta, next preceding an udātta or independent svarita, is marked by a short horizontal stroke below.

In the lexicon of Böhtlingk and Roth (also in Böhtlingk's chrestomathy) the udātta is indicated by a small Sanskrit *u* above. In transliteration the udātta is written ´, the svarita is written `.

Examples:

vípràsya (the *i* bears the udātta and therefore the *a* of the following syllable has a dependent svarita).

katháṁ rasā́yā̀ ataraḥ páyā̀ṁsi (the first syllable of *rasā́yā̀*, though immediately preceded by an udātta, has no dependent svarita, because it is also followed by an udātta).

tanvā̀ (with independent svarita, from *tanúā̀*).

svàr (with independent svarita, from *súàr*).

nadyàs (with independent svarita, from *nadíàs*).

§ 117. **Enclisis.** The principal rules about enclisis are the following:

1. The vocative is enclitic, except at the beginning of a sentence or a pāda.

2. The verbum finitum is enclitic in an independent clause,

except at the beginning of a sentence or a pāda. In a dependent clause it is accented.

3. Many particles (*ca*, *vā*, *u*, *sma*, *iva*, *cid*, *svid*, *ha* &c.) are always accentless.

4. Many forms of pronominal stems are always enclitic (*mā*, *me*, *nāu*, *nas*, *tvā*, *te*, *vām*, *vas* &c.).

Some restrictions and particularities are to be found in Whitney's grammar (§ 314 and § 591 sqq.).

Enclitic vocatives:

tvám agne vratapā́ asi.

nákir indra tvád úttaro.

ā́ tū́ na indra vṛtrahann | asmā́kam ardhám ā́ gahi.

párvatānaam | khidrám bibharṣi pṛthivi.

But:

ágne yáṁ yajñám adhvaráṁ | viçvátaḥ paribhū́r ási.

ágne náya supáthā rāyé asmā́n.

vā́yo yé te sahasríṇo | ráthāsas tébhir ā́ gahi.

yátaḥ pári jārá ivācáranti | úṣo dadṛkṣé ná púnar yatī́va.

Enclitic verbum finitum:

índraṁ víçvā avīvṛdhan | samudrávyacasaṁ gíraḥ.

agníṁ dūtáṁ vṛṇīmahe.

parjányāya prá gāyata.

asmé indrā varuṇā çárma yacchatam.

But:

gā́yanti tvā gāyatríṇo | árcanti arkám arkíṇaḥ.

gṛbhṇā́mi te sāubhagatvā́ya hástam.

índrasya nú vīríāṇi prá vocam | yā́ni cakā́ra prathamā́ni vajrī́.

ráthaṁ yé cakrúḥ suvṛ́taṁ nareṣṭhā́m.

yó gárbham óṣadhīnaam | gávāṁ kṛṇóti árvatām.

yā́su (apsú) rā́jā váruṇo yā́su sómaḥ | víçve devā́ yā́su ū́rjaṁ mádanti.

A COMPLETE LIST OF

BOOKS & PERIODICALS,

PUBLISHED AND SOLD BY

LUZAC and Co.,

Publishers to the India Office, the Asiatic Society of Bengal, the University of Chicago, etc.

(With Index)

1740

LONDON:
LUZAC & Co.
46, GREAT RUSSELL STREET (OPPOSITE THE BRITISH MUSEUM).
1898.

COMPLETE LIST OF

BOOKS AND PERIODICALS,

PUBLISHED AND SOLD BY

LUZAC and Co.

American Journal of Theology. Edited by Members of the Divinity Faculty of the University of Chicago. Vol. I. (Vol. II in progress). Quarterly. Annual Subscription. 14*s*. 6*d*.

"The theologians of America are attempting to supply a real need... it aims at a complete presentation of all recent theological work ... we give it a hearty welcome, as a scheme likely to prove of real utility to theological students and to the cause of truth." — *Guardian*.

American Journal of Semitic Languages and Literatures (continuing Hebraica). Edited by WILLIAM R. HARPER and the Staff of the Semitic Department of the University of Chicago. Vol. I—XIII. (Vol. XIV in progress). Published quarterly. Annual subscription. 14*s*.

American Journal of Sociology. Vol. I—III. (Vol. IV in progress). Published quarterly. Annual subscription. 10*s*. 6*d*.

Ánandás'rama Sanskrit Series. — Edited by Pandits of the Ánandás'rama. Published by Mahádeva Chimnáji Ápte, B.A., LL.B., Pleader High Court, and Fellow of the University of Bombay. Nos. 1 to 35. In 42 Vols. Royal 8vo. Price of the set £ 16. Single Vols. at different prices.

Asiatic Society of Bengal, Journal of. Messrs Luzac and Co are the sole agents for Great Britain and America of the Asiatic Society of Bengal and can supply the continuation of the Journal at 3*s.* each No., of the Proceedings at 1*s.* each No. As they keep a large stock of the Journal and Proceedings, they can also supply any single No. at the published price.

Assab'iniyya. — A philosophical Poem in Arabic by Mūsā B. Tūbi. Together with the Hebrew Version and Commentary styled Bāttē Hannefeš by Solomon Immānuēl Dapiera. Edited and translated by HARTWIG HIRSCHFELD. 8vo. pp. 61. 2*s.* 6*d.* net.

Assyrian and Babylonian Letters. 4 vols. See: Harper.

Aston (W. G.) — A Grammar of the Japanese Written Language. Second Edition, enlarged and improved. Roy. 8vo. Cloth. pp. 306. (Published 28*s.*) Reduced-Price, 18*s.*

Aston (W. G.) — A Short Grammar of the Japanese Spoken Language. Fourth Edition. Crown 8vo. Cloth. pp. 212. (Published 12*s.*) Reduced-Price, 7*s.* 6*d.*

Babylonian and Oriental Record. (The) — A Monthly Magazine of the Antiquities of the East. Edited by Prof. TERRIEN DE LACOUPERIE. Vol. I—VI. (Vol. VII in progress). Published monthly. Single Numbers, 1*s.* 6*d.* each.

Babylonian Magic and Sorcery. See: King.

Bāna's Kadambari. Translated, with Occasional Omissions, with a full Abstract of the Continuation of the Romance by the Author's Son Bhushanabhatta, by C. M. RIDDING. 8vo. Cloth. pp. XXIV, 232. 10*s.*

Bāna's Harsa Carita. An Historical Work, translated from the Sanskrit, by E. B. Cowell and F. W. Thomas. 8vo. Cloth. pp. XIV, 284. 10*s.*

Bezold (Ch.) — Oriental Diplomacy: being the transliterated Text of the Cuneiform Despatches between the King of Egypt and Western Asia in the XVth. century before Christ, discovered at Tell el Amarna, and now preserved in the British Museum. With full Vocabulary, grammatical Notes, &c., by CHARLES BEZOLD. Post 8vo. Cloth. pp. XLIV, 124. 18*s*. net.

"For the Assyriologist the book is a servicable and handy supplement to the British Museum volume on the Tell El-Amarna tablets. The author is specially skilled in the art of cataloguing and dictionary making and it is needless to say that he has done his work well". — *The Academy*.

"Die in dem Hauptwerke (The Tell el Amarna Tablets in the British Museum with autotype Facsimiles, etc.) vermisstte Transcription des Keilschrifttextes der Tafeln, sowie ein sehr ausführliches, mituntur die Vollständigkeit einer Concordanz erreichendes Vocabulary bietet die Oriental Diplomacy von C. Bezold, das eben deshalb gewissermassen als Schlüssel zu dem Publicationswerke betrachtet werden kann." — *Liter. Centralblatt*.

„Wichtig und sehr nützlich vor allem wegen der Einleitung und des Wörterverzeichnisses . . . Transkription und kurze Inhaltsangabe der Briefe sehr zweckmässig . . . . eine anerkennenswerthe Leistung."
Deutsche Litteraturzeitung.

Biblia. — A Monthly Magazine, devoted to Biblical Archaeology and Oriental Research. Vol. I—X. (Vol. XI in progress). Published monthly. Annual Subscription, 5*s*.

Biblical World (The) — Continuing the Old and New Testament Student. Edited by WILLIAM R. HARPER. New Series. Vol. I—X. (Vol. XI and XII in progress). Published monthly. Annual Subscription, 10*s*. 6*d*.

"The Biblical World makes a faithful record and helpful critic of present Biblical Work, as well as an efficient practical and positive independent force in stimulating and instructing the student, preacher and teacher"

Bibliographical List of Books on Africa and the East. Published in England. 2 Vols. Vol. I. Containing the Books published between the Meetings of the Eighth Oriental Congress at Stockholm, in 1889, and the Ninth Congress in London in 1892. Vol. II. Containing the Books published between the Meetings of the Ninth Oriental Congress in London, in 1892, and the Tenth Oriental Congress at Geneva, in 1894. Systematically arranged, with Preface and Author's Index, by C. G. Luzac. 12mo. each Vol. 1*s*.

Bibliotheca Indica. — Messrs Luzac & Co. are agents for the sale of this important series and keep most of the numbers in stock.

Blackden (M. W.) and G. W. Frazer. — Collection of Hieratic Graffiti, from the Alabaster Quarry of Hat-Nub, situated near Tell El Amarna. Found December 28th. 1891, copied September, 1892. Obl. pp. 10. 10*s*.

Buddhaghosuppatti; or, Historical Romance of the Rise and Career of Buddaghosa. Edited and translated by JAMES GRAY, Professor of Pali. Rangoon College. Two Parts in one. Demy 8vo. Cloth. pp. VIII, 75 and 36. 6*s*.

Budge (E. A. Wallis) — The Laughable Stories collected by Bar-Hebraeus. The Syriac Text with an English Translation, by E. A. WALLIS BUDGE, Litt. D., F. S. A., Keeper of the Department of Egyptian and Assyrian Antiquities, British Museum. 8vo. Cloth. 21*s*. net. [Luzac's Semitic Texts and Translation Series, Vol. I].

"Dr. BUDGE's book will be welcome as a handy reading book for advanced students of Syriac, but in the mean time the stories will be an addition to the literature of gnomes and proverbs, of which so many are found in India, and in Persian, Hebrew and Arabic, although not yet published. We are happy to say that Dr. BUDGE's new book is well edited and translated as far as we can judge". — *Athenæum*.

"The worthy Syrian Bishops idea of humour may excite admiration when we hear that he collected his quips in the grey dawn of the middle ages". — *Pall Mall Gazette*.

"Man sieht, das Buch ist in mehr als einer Hinsicht interessant, und wir sind Budge für die Herausgabe aufrichtig dankbar. — *Lit. Centralb.*

"Sous le titre de *Récits amusants*, le célèbre polygraphe syrien Barhébraeus a réuni une collection de sept cent vingt-sept contes, divisés en vingt chapitres et renfermant des aphorismes, des anecdotes et des fables d'animaux ayant un caractère soit moral, soit simplement récréatif. Le livre nous était connu par quelques spécimens publiés précédement. M. BUDGE, qui a déja rendu tant de services aux lettres syriaques, vient d'éditer l'ouvrage entier avec une traduction anglaise..... En tous cas, M. B. a eu raison de ne pas faire un choix et de donner l'ouvrage en son entier.... Les aphorismes, écrits dans un style concis et avec, une pointe dont la finesse n'est pas toujours sensible, présentent des difficultés de traduction dont M. B. a généralement triomphé." — *Revue Critique.*

"È questo un libro singolare, appartemente ad un genere assai scarso nella letteratura siriaca, quantunque così ricca, cioè a quello dell'amena letteratura. Bar Ebreo scrisse questo libro nella vecchiaia, o forse allora mise insieme e ordinò estr atti che avea prese nelle lunghe letture da lui fatte, di tanto opere e cosi svariate.... I cultori degli studi siriaci saranno assai grati al Dr. Budge per questo suo novello contributo; l'edizione per carte e per tipi è veramente bellissima." — *La Cultura.*

Budge, see Luzac's Semitic Text and Translation Series. Vols. I, III, V and VII.

Cappeller (Carl) — A Sanskrit-English Dictionary. Based upon the St. Petersburg Lexicons. Royal 8vo. Cloth. pp. VIII, 672 [Published £ 1. 1*s*]. Reduced to 10*s*. 6*d*.

"Linguistic and other students should hail with satisfaction the publication of a cheap and handy Sanskrit-English Dictionary, such as is now to be found in the new English edition of Prof. CAPPELLER's Sanskrit-German 'Wörterbuch,' recently published by Messrs. Luzac. The book is well adapted to the use of beginners, as it specially deals with the text usually read in commencing Sanskrit; but it will be of use also to philological students — or such as have mastered the Nāgari character — as it includes most Vedic words, a great desideratum in many earlier dictionaries, especially such as were founded on native sources. The basis of the present work is, on the contrary, the great lexicon of Boethlingk and Roth with the addition of compound forms likely to be of service to beginners." — *Athenæum.*

"The English edition of Prof. CAPPELLER's Sanskrit Dictionary is some thing more than a mere translation of the German edition. It includes the vocabulary of several additional texts; many compounds have been inserted which are not given in the Petersburg lexicons; and some improvements have been made in the arrangement. The errors enumerated by the reviewer of the *Academy* have for the most part been corrected, though a few still remain. .... The book is certainly the cheapest, and, for a beginner, in some respects the best, of existing Sanskrit-English dictionaries." — *Academy.*

"Professor CAPPELLER furnishes the Student of Sanskrit, if not with a complete Lexicon, — for that he tells us, was not his object, — still with a handy and yet very full vocabulary of all the words occurring in the texts which are generally studied in that language. His plan is to avoid all unnecessary complications, to give each word in such a manner as to show its formation, if it is not itself a stem. It is not merely an English version of the author's Sanskrit-German Dictionary, nor merely an enlarged edition of the same; it is a new work, with a distinct plan and object of its own. We can recommend it to the Sanskrit student as a sufficient dictionary for all practical purposes, which will enable him to dispense with larger and more costly and complicated Lexicons till he has acquired a considerable proficiency in this difficult and scientific language." — *Asiatic Quarterly Review.*

Ceylon. A Tale of Old..... See: Sinnatamby.

Chakrabarti (J. Ch.) — The Native States of India. 8vo. Cloth. pp. XIV, 274. With Map. 5*s.* net.

Cool (W.) — **With the Dutch in the East.** An Outline of the Military Operations in Lombock, 1894, Giving also a Popular Account of the Native Characteristics, Architecture, Methods of Irrigations, Agricultural Pursuits, Folklore, Religious Customs and a History of the Introduction of Islamism and Hinduism into the Island. By Capt. W. COOL (Dutch Engineer), Knight of the Order of Orange Nassau; decorated for important War Services in the Dutch Indies; Professor at the High School of War, the Hague. Translated from the Dutch by E. J. Taylor. Illustrated by G. B. HOOYER. Late Lieut. Col. of the Dutch Indian Army; Knight of the Military Order of William; decorated for important War Services in the Dutch Indies. Roy. 8vo. Cloth. 21*s.*

"There are, it is to be feared, but few books published in this country from which English readers can obtain information as to the doings of the Dutch in their Eastern colonies. — For this reason we are glad that Capt. Cool's account of the Lombock expedition has been translated." — *Athenæum.*

"The book contains an interesting account of the Balinese and Sassak customs, and throws some light on the introduction of the Mahomedan and Hindu religions into Lombock ... The translation by Miss E. J. Taylor is satisfactory, and some of the illustrations are excellent." — *The Times.*

"Lombock forms a small link in the long chain of volcanic lands ... To folklorists and students of primitive religions it has always presented many attractive features ... They will be much interested in the local traditions recorded in the volume before us. Miss Taylor's version deserves a word of recognition, and the general equipment of the book is creditable to the Amsterdam press. There is a good index." — *Academy.*

"The author not only describes the military operations, but gives a full history of Lombock and its people. Much curious information as to a land very much out of the way and little known to English readers is given. In addition the account of the actual warfare is full of incident. The book is freely illustrated." — *Yorkshire Daily Post.*

"This is a work which will no doubt attract considerable attention, both in the West and throughout the East. Miss Taylor has acquitted herself as a translator with rare ability and taste, and the comprehensive and excellent way in which the work is illustrated adds an additional charm to what is at once the most entertaining and most attractive chapter of Netherlands Indian history." — *European Mail.*

"Besides containing a great deal of information concerning this hitherto very slightly known island and its inhabitants, Captain Cool's volume is profusely and excellently illustrated ... Miss Taylor's translation of it is fluent and thoroughly readable." — *Glasgow Herald.*

Cowell, E. B., See: Bāna's Harsa Carita.

Cowper (B. H.) Principles of Syriac Grammar. Translated and abridged from the work of Dr. HOFFMANN. 8vo. Cloth. pp. 184. *7s. 6d.*

Cust (R. N.) — The Gospel Message or Essays, Addresses, Suggestions and Warnings of the different aspects of Christian Missions to Non Christian Races and peoples. 8vo. pp. 494. Paper *6s. 6d.* Cloth. *7s. 6d.*

".... There are few objects of controversy in missionary matters which are not very fully discussed by Dr. CUST, and if we not infrequently differ from him we gladly thank him for copious information and the benefits of his long experience". — *Guardian.*

"It is a big book. it ranges over a very wide field, and it is never dull or dry". — *Expository Times.*

"The scheme is so comprehensive as to include almost every detail of the missionary enterprise. Every essay is stamped, of course with the personality of its author, whose views are expressed with characteristie force and clearness". — *The Record.*

Cust (R. N.) — **Essay on the Common Features which appear in all Forms of Religious belief.** Post 8vo. Cloth. pp. XXIV, 194. *5s.*

"Dr. CUST has put his very considerable knowledge to excellent purposes in this modest little publication. He seems most at home with the faiths of the East, but even the most elementary of savage creeds have not escaped him". — *Pall Mall Gazette.*

Cust (R. N.) — Essay on Religious Conceptions. Post 8vo. Cloth. pp. V, 148. *5s.*

Cust (R. N.) — Linguistic and Oriental Essays. Fourth Series. From 1861 to 1895. 8vo. pp. XXV, 634. Paper Covers. *16s.*, Cloth. *17s. 6d.*

Dawlatshah's Lives of the Persian Poets. Edited by EDWARD G. BROWNE, Lecturer in Persian in the University of Cambridge. Vol. 1. Tadhkiratu'sh Sh'arā. 8vo. Cloth. *18s.* net.

Edkins (Joseph) — China's Place in Philology. An Attempt to show that the Languages of Europe and Asia have a common Origin. Demy 8vo. Cloth. pp. XXIII, 403. (Published *10s. 6d.*) *7s. 6d.*

Edkins (Joseph) — Introduction to the Study of the Chinese Characters. Royal 8vo. Boards. pp. XIX, 211, 101. (Published *18s.*) *12s. 6d.*

Edkins (Joseph) — Nirvana of the Northern Buddhists. 8vo. pp. 21. Reprint. *6d.*

Edkins (Joseph) — Chinese Architecture. Contents. — 1. Classical Style. — 2. Post-Confucian Style. — 3. Buddhist Style. — 4. Modern Style. 8vo. pp. 36. *1s.*

Edkins (Joseph) — Chinese Currency. Roy. 8vo. pp. 29. *1s.*

Edkins (Joseph) — Ancient Symbolism among the Chinese. Cr. 8vo. pp. 26. *6d.*

Efes Damîm. — A Series of Conversations at Jerusalem between a Patriarch of the Greek Church and a Chief Rabbi of the Jews, concerning the Malicious Charge against the Jews of using Christian Blood. By J. B. LEVINSOHN. Translated from the Hebrew by Dr. L. LOEWE. Roy. 8vo. Cloth. pp. XVI, 208. (Published *8s.*) Reduced Price *2s. 6d.*

Eitel (E. J.) — Europe in China. The History of Hongkong. From the Beginning to the year 1882. 8vo. Cloth. pp. VII, 575. With Index. *15s.* net.

"His work rises considerably above the level commonly attained by colonial histories written from a colonial point of view". — *Times.*

"His painstaking volume is really a detailed history of the colony and of the adminstration of successive governors from 1841 down to the present day". — *Daily Telegraph.*

"This is an interesting book. The subject is full of matter, and Dr. EITEL has, as a rule, treated it successfully. — *Athenæum.*

".... The student will find Dr. EITEL's book a very storehouse of information.... has told it with a mastery of fact that vouches for his industry and perseverance" — *Saturday Review.*

Gladstone (Right Hon. W. E.) — Archaic Greece and the East. 8vo. pp. 32. 1*s.*

Gribble (J. D. B.) — A History of the Deccan. With numerous Illustrations, Plates, Portraits, Maps and Plans. Vol. I. Roy. 8vo. Cloth. 21*s.*

„In a style easy and pleasant the author tells the story of the Mohammedan occupation of the Deccan .... the general style of the book and the admirable photographs and drawings with which it is enriched leave nothing to be desired" — *Athenæum.*

"Mr. J. D. B. GRIBBLE has accomplished a difficult task. He has constructed from original materials a continuous narrative of one of the most confused periods of Indian history. He has also presented it with a lucidity of style which will go far to render it acceptable to the reading public.... The book is illustrated by a number of interesting reproductions of scenery and architecture in Southern India. These and the maps, plans, and clear genealogical tables reflect credit both upon the author and the publisher". — *Times.*

"Mr. GRIBBLE has brought great industry and knowledge of the country to this compilation .... The work is of some historical importance". — *Saturday Review.*

Gray (James). See Buddhaghosuppatti.

Gray (James). See Jinalankara.

Guide to the Dutch East Indies. By Dr. J. F van BEMMELEN and G. B. HOOYER. Trans. from the Dutch by the Rev. B. J. BERRINGTON B.A., with 16 Plates, 13 Maps and Plans, and a copious index. Sm. 8vo. pp. 202. 1*s.* 6*d.*

"For any one going in that direction this remarkably complete little work is indispensable". — *Pall Mall Gazette.*

"The guide book omits nothing needed by the traveller. It describes the necessary outfit, customs afloat and ashore, mode of living, how to dress, how often to bathe, who to tip, and how much". — *The Shipping World.*

Guirandon (F. G. de) — Manuel de la langue foule, parlée dans la Sénégambie et le Soudan. Grammaire textes, vocabulaire. 8vo. Cloth. pp. 144. 6*s*.

Halcombe (Charles J. H.) — **The Mystic Flowery Land.** A Personal Narrative. By CHARLES J. H. HALCOMBE. Late of Imperial Customs. China, 8vo. Cloth. gilt. pp. 226. 16*s*.

"This valuable and handsome volume contains thirty long chapters, a frontispiece of the Author and his wife — the latter in her Oriental costume — numerous fine reproductions from photographs, and several beautiful coloured pictures representing many scenes and phases of Chinese life, etchings and comprehensive notes by the Author.

"His pages are full of incident and his narrative often vivid and vigorous". — *Times.*

"The illustrations are good and numerous. Many are facsimiles of coloured Chinese drawings showing various industrial occupations: others are photogravures representing buildings and scenery". — *Morning Post.*

"Handsomely attired in red, yellow and gold, with Chinese characters to give further appropriateness to the outer garb, is this volume of freely illustrated personal experience in China.... Mr. HALCOMBE gives a graphic description of places and peoples, with their manners and customs". — *Liverpool Courier.*

"The illustrations are all good, and the Chinese pictures reproduced in colours interesting. We have not seen any of them before". — *Westminster Review.*

Hansei Zasshi. Monthly. Vol. I—XII. (Vol. XIII in progress). Annual subscription. 6*s*.

Hardy (R. Spence) — **The Legends and theories of the Buddhists.** Compared with History and Science. 8vo. Cloth. pp. 244. 7*s*. 6*d*.

Harîri. — The Assemblies of al Harîri. Translated from the Arabic with an Introduction and notes, Historical and Grammatical, by TH. CHENERY and F. STEINGASS. With Preface and Index, by F. F. ARBUTHNOT, 2 Vols. 8vo. Cloth. pp. X, 540 and XI, 395. £ 1.10*s*.

Harper (Robert Francis) — **Assyrian and Babylonian Letters,** belonging to the K. Collection of the British Museum. By ROBERT FRANCIS HARPER, of the University of Chicago. Vols. I to IV. Post 8vo. Cloth. Price of each Vol. £ 1. 5*s*. net.

"The Assyriologist, will welcome them with gratitude, for they offer him a mass of new material which has been carefully copied and well printed, and which cannot fail to yield important results." — *Athenæum.*

"The book is well printed, and it is a pleasure to read the texts given in it, with their large type and ample margin." — *Academy.*

Hebraica. — A Quarterly Journal in the Interests of Semitic Study. Edited by WILLIAM R. HARPER and the Staff of the Semitic Department of the University of Chicago. Vol. I—XI. Published quarterly. Annual Subscription. 14*s.*

See American Journal of Semitic Languages, etc.

India. (The Native States of). See: Chakrabarti.

India. (The Armenians in). See: Seth.

Indian Antiquary (The) — A Journal of Oriental Research in Archaeology, Epigraphy, etc. etc. Edited by R. C. TEMPLE. Vol. I—XXVI. (Vol. XXVII in progress). Annual Subscription, £ 1. 16*s.*

Indian Terms. (A Glossary of). See: Temple.

Indian Wisdom. See: Monier-Williams.

Jastrow's Dictionary of the Targumim, the Talmud Babli and Yerushalmi, and the Midrashic Literature. Compiled by M. JASTROW, Ph. D. Parts I to IX. 4to. pp. 480. 5*s.* each Part.

"This is the only Talmudic dictionary in English, and all students should subscribe to it. The merits of this work are now too well known to need repetition." — *Jewish Chronicle.*

Jinalankara or **"Embellishments of Buddha"**, by Buddharakkhita. Edited with Introduction, Notes and Translation, by JAMES GRAY. Two Parts in one. Demy 8vo. Cloth. 6*s.*

"The commendable care with which the volume has been prepared for the use of students is evident throughout its pages. — *Athenæum.*

Johnson (Capt. F. N). — The Seven Poems etc. See: Muallakat.

Johnston (C.) Useful Sanskrit Nouns and Verbs. In English Letters. Compiled by CHARLES JOHNSTON,

Bengal Civil Service, Dublin University Sanskrit Prizeman, India Civil Service Sanskrit Prizeman. Small 4to. Boards. pp. 30. 2*s*. 6*d*.

Johnston (C.) — The Awakening to the Self. Translated from the Sanskrit of Shankara the Master. Oblong 8vo. Paper covers. 2*s*.

Journal of the Buddhist Text Society of India. Edited by Sarat Candra Das, C. J. E. Vols. I to IV. 8vo. Calcutta, 1893—1897. £ 1. 10*s*.

Messrs. Luzac & Co. are the English agents for the above and can supply the Continuation. Subscription. 10*s*. each Vol.

Judson (A.) — English-Burmese Dictionary. Fourth Edition. Royal 8vo. Half bound. pp. 1752. £ 1. 12*s*.

Judson (A.) — Burmese-English Dictionary. Revised and enlarged by ROBERT C. STEVENSON. Royal 8vo. Paper covers. pp. 1192.

Kathákoça. See Tawney.

King (Leonard W.) — Babylonian Magic and Sorcery. Being "The Prayers of the Lifting of the Hand". The Cuneiform Texts of a Group of Babylonian and Assyrian Incantations and magical Formulae, edited with Transliterations, Translations, and full Vocabulary from Tablets of the Kuyunjik Collection preserved in the British Museum. By LEONARD W. KING, M. A., Assistant in the Department of Egyptian and Assyrian Antiquities, British Museum. Roy. 8vo. Cloth. 18*s*. net.

"We cannot pretend to form an adequate judgment of the merits of Mr. KING's work, but it is manifestly conceived and executed in a very scholarly spirit." — *Times*.

"Mr. KING's book, will, we believe be of great use to all students of Mesopotamian religions, and it marks an era in Assyriological studies in England.... A word of special praise is due to Mr. KING for the excellence of his autograph plates of text." — *Athenæum*.

"The work will be found a valuable addition to our knowledge of Babylonian history, and to the study of comparative philology."

Morning Post.

King, L. W. See: Luzac's Semitic Text and Translation Series, Vols. II, IV and VI.

Kittel (Rev. F.) — A Kannada-English Dictionary. By Rev. F. KITTEL, B. G. E. M. Royal 8vo. Half-Bound. pp. L. 1725. £ 1. 12*s.*

Korean Repository. Vols. I to III. Annual Subscription 15*s.* Post free.

Land (J. P. N.) — The Principles of Hebrew Grammar. By J. P. N. LAND, Professor of Logic and Metaphysics in the University of Leyden. Translated from the Dutch by REGINALD LANE POOLE, Balliol College, Oxford. Demy 8vo. Cloth. pp. XX, 219 (Published 7*s.* 6*d.*) Reduced price 5*s.*

Lives of the Persian Poets Series. See Dawlatshah.

Loewe (L.) — A Dictionary of the Circassian Language. In two Parts. English—Circassian—Turkish, and Circassian—English—Turkish. 8vo. Cloth. (Published 21*s.*) Reduced price 6*s.*

Loewe (L.) Efes Damim. See: Efes.

Luzac's Oriental List. — Containing Notes and News on, and a Bibliographical List of all new Publications on Africa and the East. Published Monthly. Annual Subscription, 3*s.* Vols. I to VIII (1890—1897) are still to be had (with Index, half-bound), at £ 2. 15*s.*

Vols. I to IV are nearly out of print and can only be sold in the set. Vols V to VIII are still to be had at 5*s.* each vol.

"It deserves the support of Oriental students. Besides the catalogue of new books published in England, on the Continent, in the East, and in America, it gives, under the heading of "Notes and News" details about important Oriental works, which are both more full and more careful than anything of the sort to be found elsewhere." — *Academy.*

"A bibliographical monthly publication which should be better known." *The Record.*

Luzac's Semitic Text and Translation Series. Vol. I: See: Budge.

Vol. II. The Letters and Despatches of Hammurabi king of Babylon about B. C. 2250, to Sin-idinnam, King of Larsa, together with other royal and official correspondence of the same period: the Cuneiform texts edited with an Introduction and short descriptions by L. W. King, M. A.

This volume will contain about 100 letters relating to a variety of official subjects, and their contents are of great importance for the study of the history of Babylonia, Elam and the neighbouring districts about the time of the patriarch Abraham. These letters reveal the system by which Hammurabi maintained his rule in the remote provinces of his newly acquired empire, and contain some of the orders and directions which he issued for the movements of troops, for the building of canals and waterways, for the food-supply of his capital, and for the regulation of legal tribunals. The letters of Hammurabi are the oldest Babylonian despatches extant. — *Ready in June.*

Vol. III. The History of the Blessed Lady Mary the Virgin, and the History of the Image of Christ, which the men of Tiberias made to mock at; the Syriac text edited, with an English translation, by E. A. Wallis Budge, Litt. D., D. Lit., etc. — *Ready in October.*

This Life of the Virgin is the fullest known to exist in Syriac, and varies in many important particulars from the versions of which fragments have already been published. The Life has been copied from an ancient Nestorian MS., to the text of which have been added all the variants found in the XVIth century MS. in the possession of the Royal Asiatic Society of Great Britain.

Vol. IV. The Letters and Despatches of Hammurabi together with other official and private correspondence of the same period, by L. W. King, M. A.

This volume will contain a number of transliterations and translations of the texts of the 100 letters and despatches which are printed in volume 2; to these will be added indexes of proper names etc. and a List of Characters. An attempt will be made to give a description of the circumstances under which these letters were written, and short notes on points of grammar, history, etc. will be added. — *In the Press.*

Vol. V. The History of Rabban Hormizd by Mâr Simon, the disciple of Mâr Yôzâdhâḳ; the Syriac text edited, with an English translation by E. A. Wallis Budge, Litt. D., D. Lit., etc.

The text describes the life of this famous Nestorian anchorite, the building of his monastery, and the struggle which went on in the VIIth century between the rival sects of Jacobites and Nestorians in Mesopotamia. This prose version of the life of Rabban Hormizd is, probably, the source from which the metrical versions were drawn; and it is of great importance for the study of the second great development of monasticism in Mesopotamia. — *In the Press.*

Vol. VI. Babylonian Private Letters written during the period of the First Dynasty of Babylon; the Cuneiform texts edited with Introduction and short descriptions by L. W. King, M. A.

This volume will contain about 200 letters of a private nature which reveal the social condition of the country and incidentally throw much light upon the civilization of the period. From grammatical and lexicographical points of view these texts are of considerable importance, for they afford numerous examples of unusual words and forms of expression. — *In the Press.*

Vol. VII. The Life of Rabban Bar-Idtâ by John his disciple; The Syrac text edited, with an English translation, by E. A. WALLIS BUDGE, Litt. D., D. Lit., etc.

Bar-Idtâ was the founder of a famous rule and monastery in Mesopotamia in the VIIth century, and the author of a verv valuable work on monastic history which is quoted with respect by Thomas, Bishop of Margâ. He was a contemporary of Babhai of Mount Izlâ, and of Jacob of Bêth Abbê.

Volumes 5, 6, and 7 will, it is hoped be ready early next year.

Macnaghten (Sir W. Hay) — Principle of Hindu and Mohammedan Law. Republished from the Principles and Precedences of the same. Edited by the late H. H. WILSON. 8vo. Cloth. pp. 240. 6*s*.

Margoliouth (D. S.) — Arabic Papyri of the Bodleian Library reproduced by the Collotype Process. With Transcription and Translation. Text in 4to. pp. 7 and 2 Facsimiles in large folio. 5*s*.

Margoliouth (D. S.) — Chrestcmathia Baidawiana. The Commentary of El-Baidâwi on Sura III. Translated and explained for the Use of Students of Arabic. By D. S. MARGOLIOUTH, M. A., Laudian Professor of Arabic in the University of Oxford, etc. etc. Post 8vo. Cloth. 12*s*.

"The book is as scholarly as it is useful. Of particular importance are the numerous grammatical annotations which give the beginner an insight into the method of the Arabic national grammarians, and which form an excellent preparatory study for the perusal of these works in the original..... The introduction and the remarks in particular show how well Mr. MARGOLIOUTH has mastered the immense literatures of Moslim Tradition, Grammar and Kalam.... The perusal of the book affords pleasure from beginning to end." — *Journal Royal Asiatic Society.*

Mirkhond. — The Rauzat-us-Safa; or, Garden of Purity. Translated from the Original Persian by E. REHATSEK; edited by F. F. ARBUTHNOT. Vols. I to V. 10*s*. each Vol.

Vols. 1 and 2 contain: The Histories of Prophets, Kings and Khalifs.
Vols. 3 and 4 contain: The life of Muhammad the Apostle of Allah.
Vol. 5 contains: The Lives of Abú Bakr, O'mar, O'thmàn, and Ali', the four immediate successors of Muhammad the Apostle.

Monier-Williams (Sir Monier) — Indian Wisdom; or Examples of the religious, philosophical, and ethical Doctrines of the Hindus, with a brief History of the chief Departments of Sanskrit Literature, and some account of the past and present Condition of India, moral and intellectual. By Sir MONIER MONIER-WILLIAMS, K. C. I. E., M. A., Hon. D. C. L., Oxford. Fourth Edition, enlarged and improved. Post 8vo. Cloth. pp. 575. £ 1. 1*s.*

"His book .... still remains indispensable for the growing public, which seeks to learn the outline of Indian literature and thought in a simple and readable form. We are glad to welcome the fourth edition of this eminently readable book." — *Daily Chronicle.*

"The learned professor's thorough mastery of his subject enables him to deal effectively with his difficult task. .... He omits nothing that enters the scope of his work: he is choice in his selections and accurate in his comments, and the result is a work as instructive and sound as it is pleasant to read." — *Asiatic Quarterly Review.*

"For all students of the philosophy of religion, as well as for all especially interested in Indian literature and thought, the work is one of very great value." — *Glasgow Herald.*

"It is a fine volume and contains valuable additions by the author.... this edition will be more than ever prized by students of Indian lore." *Scotsman.*

Muallakat. — The Seven Poems suspended in the Temple at Mecca. Translated from the Arabic. By Capt. F. E. JOHNSON. With an Introduction by Shaikh Taizullabhai. 8vo. pp. XXIV, 238. 7*s.* 6*d.*

"This handy volume decidedly supplies a great want for those who make a serious study of Arabic .... The grammatical, historical, geographical and other notes comments and explanations are ample and thorough". — *Imperial and Asiatic Quarterly Review.*

Müller (F. Max) — Address delivered at the Opening of the Ninth International Congress of Orientalists, held in London, Sept. 5, 1892, 8vo. pp. 66. 1*s.* 6*d.*

Mystic Flowery Land. See: Halcombe.

Oriental Translation Fund (New), See: Mirkhond, Tawney, Bana, and Harîri.

Oudemans Jzn. (A. C.) — The Great Sea-Serpent. An historical and critical Treatise. With the Reports of 187 Appearances (including those of the Appendix), the Suppositions and Suggestions of scientific and non-scientific Persons, and the Author's Conclusions. With 82 Illustrations. Royal 8vo. Cloth. pp. XV, 592. £ 1. 5*s*. net.

"The volume is extremely interesting" *Athenaeum.*

Reis Sidi Ali. The Travels and Adventures of the Turkish Admiral. In India, Afghanistan, Central Asia and Persia 1553—1556. Translated from the Turkish into English with notes. By H. VAMBERY. — *In the Press.*

Ridding (C. M.) — See: Bana's Kadambari.

Rosen (F.) — A Modern Persian Colloquial Grammar, containing a short Grammar, Dialogues and Extracts from Nasir Eddin Shah's Diaries, Tales, etc. and a Vocabulary. Cr. 8vo. Cloth. pp. XIV, 400. 10*s*. 6*d*,

"Dr. ROSEN's learned work will be useful to all who have occasion to go to Persia, Baluchistan, and Afghanistan. The Vocabulary will be a boon to students, especially as it is in the same volume with the grammar and the dialogues." — *Publ. Circular.*

"Very useful to students." — *Westminster Review.*

"Excellent Guide to the acquisition of Persian." — *Asiatic Quarterly Review.*

Rosthorn (A. de) — On the Tea Cultivation in Western Ssüch'uan and the Tea Trade with Tibet via Tachienlu. 8vo. pp. 40. With Sketch Map. 2*s*. net.

Ruben (Paul) — Critical Remarks upon some Passages of the Old Testament, by PAUL RUBEN, Ph. D. 4to. Cloth. pp. II. 24, 14. 3*s*. 6*d*.

"It may suffice to congratulate ourselves that a scholar of vigorous mind and accurate philological training is devoting his leisure to a subject worthy of attention .... Very many of the notes are in a high degree stimulating and suggestive. The get up of the book is excellent" *Academy.*

"Dr. RUBEN shows much originality, a wide knowledge of authorities, and a true grasp of critical principles". — *Jewish Chronicle.*

Sacred Books of the Old Testament. — A critical Edition of the Hebrew Text, Printed in Colours, with Notes. Prepared by eminent Biblical Scholars of Europe and America. Under the editorial direction of PAUL HAUPT, Professor in the John Hopkins Univ. Baltimore. **Edition de Luxe,** in 120 numbered Copies only. 4to. Subscription price for the complete Work (20 Parts), £ 20.

Prospectuses sent on application. The following Parts have already been issued:

Part 1: **Book of Genesis,** by C. J. Ball. pp. 120. London. 1896. £ 2.
Part 3: **Leviticus,** by Prof. S. R. Driver. pp. 32. 1894. 16*s*.
Part 6: **Joshua,** by Prof. W. H. Bennet. pp. 32. 1895. £ 1.
Part 8: **Samuel,** by Prof. K. Budde. pp. 100. 1894. £ 1. 10*s*.
Part 11: **Jeremiah,** by Prof. C. H. Cornill. pp. 80. 1895. £ 1.
Part 14: **Psalms,** by J. Wellhausen, pp. 96. 1895. £ 1. 10*s*.
Part 18: **Book of Daniel,** by A. Kamphausen, 4to. pp. 44. 1896. £ 1.
Part 20: **Chronicles,** by R. Kittel. pp. 82. 1895. £ 1. 10*s*.

A valuable "Edition de Luxe" in 120 numbered copies only, and which may be described as the most splendidly got up Hebrew work in existence.

Each single part is numbered and signed by the editor with his own hand. The single parts will be issued in highly elegant covers. After the conclusion of the work a handsome binding cover will be supplied.

Sankaranarayana (P.) — **English-Telugu Dictionary,** by P. SANKARANARAYNA M. A., M. R. A. S., Tutor to their Highnesses the Princes of Cochin. 8vo. Cloth. pp. 61, 756, 10*s*. 6*d*.

Sanskrit Phonetics. A Manual of. See: Uhlenbeck.

Sanskrit Nouns and Verbs. See: Johnston.

Sayce (A. H.) — **Address** to the Assyrian Section of the Ninth International Congress of Orientalists. 8vo. pp. 32. 1*s*.

Sauerwein (G.) — **A Pocket Dictionary** of the English and Turkish Languages. Small 8vo. Cloth. limp. pp. 298. 3*s*. 6*d*.

Scholia on passages of the Old Testament. By MAX JACOB Bishop of Edessa. Now first edited in the original Syriac with an English translation and notes by G. PHILLIP. DD. 8vo. Paper Covers. 5*s.*

Seth (Mesrovb J.) — History of the Armenians in India. From the earliest Times to the present Day. 8vo. Cloth. pp. XXIV, 199. 7*s.* 6*d.* net.

"The subject is invested with peculiar interest at the present time by recent events in Asia Minor .... his unpretending little work is a valuable reportory of original information never before accessible in print and scarcely even known to exist." — *Times.*

"The book is happily distinguished among the number of books recently issued concerning Armenia in that it deals strictly with fact..... The volume deserves the attention of every one interested in the history of India and of the hardly treated race which seems to flourish better there than in its own country." — *Scotsman.*

"Sinnatamby". Letchimey. A Tale of Old Ceylon. 8vo. pp. III, 54. With Photogr. Plates and Illustrations. *In the Press.*

Stein (M. A.) — Catalogue of the Sanskrit MSS. in the Raghunata Temple Library of His Highness the Maharaja of Jammu and Kashmir. 4to. Cloth. pp. 423. 12*s.*

Steele's (R.) The Discovery of Secrets, attributed to Geber from the MS Arabic text. 8vo. 1*s.*

Stoffel (C.) Studies in English, Written and Spoken. For the Use of continental Students. With Index. First Series. Roy. 8vo. Cloth. pp. XII, 332. 7*s.* 6*d.*

Suhrillekha (The); or **"Friendly Letter;"** written by Lung Shu (Nàgàrjuna), and addressed to King Sadvaha. Translated from the Chinese Edition of I-Tsing, by the late Rev. SAMUEL BEAL, with the Chinese Text. 8vo. pp. XIII, 51. 5*s.*

Swami Vivekananda's Addresses. See: Vivekananda.

Tawney (C. H.) — The Kathákoça; or **Treasury of Stories.** Translated from Sanskrit Manuscripts. With Appendix, containing Notes, by Prof. ERNST LEUMANN. 8vo. Cloth. pp. XXIII, 260. 10*s.*

Temple (G.) — A Glossary of Indian Terms relating to Religion, Customs, Government, Land, and other Terms and Words in Common Use. To which is added a Glossary of Terms used in District Work in the N. W. Provinces and Oudh., and also of those applied to Labourers. With an Appendix giving Computation of Time and Money, and Weights and Measures, in British India, and Forms of Address. Roy. 8vo. Cloth. pp. IV, 332. *7s. 6d.*

"The book is moderate in price and clear in print." — *Athenæum.*

"The book is handy, well printed and well got up and no student of Indian subjects should be without it." — *Asiatic Quarterly Review.*

"Students of Oriental travel may find something servicable in its pages; and those who are engaged in trade in the East Indies might occasionally turn to the volume, with profit, if it were on the office shelf." — *The Nation.*

Temple (Major R. C.) — **Notes on Antiquities in Ramannadesa.** (The Talaing Country of Burma.) 4to. pp. 40. With 24 Plates and a Map. *18s.*

Thomas, F. W., See: Bāna, Harsa Carita.

Tiele (C. P.) — **Western Asia,** according to the Most Recent Discoveries. Rectorial Address on the Occasion of the 318th Anniversary of the Leyden University, 8th February, 1893. Translated by ELIZABETH J. TAYLOR. Small 8vo. Bound. pp. 36. *2s. 6d.*

"An authoritative summary of the results of recent Oriental research and discovery." — *The Times.*

"The address presents a graphic picture of the political situation in Western Asia in the fifteenth and fourteenth centuries B. C."

Morning Post.

"The professor's grasp of his subject is very evident, and his deductions from the materials commented on worthy of all attention."

Imperial and Asiatic Quarterly Review.

T'oung Pao. — **Archives pour servir à l'étude de l'histoire,** des langues, de la géographie et de l'ethnographie de l'Asie orientale. (Chine, Japon, Corée, Indo-Chine, Asie Centrale et Malaise.) Rédigées par MM. G. SCHLEGEL et H. CORDIER. Vol. I—VIII. Vol. IX in progress). Annual Subscription. £ 1

Transactions of the Ninth International Congress of Orientalists. London, 5th to 12th September, 1892.) Edited by E. DELMAR MORGAN. 2 Vols. Roy. 8vo. Cloth. £ 1. 15 *s*.

Vol. I. contains: Indian and Aryan Sections. £ 1. 1*s*.

Vol. II. contains: Semitic, Egypt and Africa, Geographical, Archaic Greece and the East, Persia and Turkey, China, Central Asia and the Far East, Australasia, Anthropology and Mythology Sections. £ 1. 1*s*.

Uhlenbeck. (C. C.). A Manual of Sanskrit Phonetics. In comparison with the Indogermanic mother-language, for students of Germanic and classical philology. 8vo. pp. 115. 6*s*.

Ummagga Yataka. See: Yatawara.

Usha. — The Dawn. A Vedic Periodical, edited by Pandit Satya Vrata Samasrami. 8vo. Published monthly. Annual subscription. £ 1. 1*s*.

Valmiki. — The Ramayan of Valmiki. Translated into English Verse, by R. T. H. GRIFFITH, M. A., C. I. E. Complete in one Volume. 8vo. Cloth. pp. IX, 576. 7*s*. 6*d*.

Vambery, see: Reis Sidi Ali.

Vivekânanda (Swami). — Lectures delivered in London. Nos. 1—12. 6*d*. each.

Vivekânanda (Swami). — Madras Lectures. 8vo. 1*s*. 6*d*.

Vizianagram Sanskrit Series. — Under the Superintendence of ARTHUR VENIS, M.A., Oxon, Principal, Sanskrit College, Benares. Different Prices.

West (Sir Raymond) — Higher Education in India: Its Position and Claims. 8vo. pp. 61. 1892. 1*s*.

Wildeboer (G.) — The Origin of the Canon of of the Old Testament. An historico-critical Enquiry. Translated by WISNER BAÇON. Edited with

Preface by Prof. GEORGE F. MOORE. Royal 8vo. Cloth. pp. XII, 182. *7s. 6d.*

"We will only add that we cordially echo the professor's hope that his book may not only be read by professed students but that it may come also into the hands of such as have already left the University."
Guardian.

"The method adopted is that of historical investigation: the student is thus enabled to see how the results of critical inquiry have been obtained .... he accompanies a guide who is familiar with the way which leads to them." — *Academy.*

"The first thing to notice is the translation. This is how a book ought to be translated .... The book must be used, not read merely ... it is independent, painstaking, farseeing." — *Expository Times.*

Winckler (H.) — The Tell-El-Amarna Letters. Transliteration, English Translation, Vocabulary, etc. Roy. 8vo. Cloth. pp. XLII, 416, and Registers 50 pages. £ 1. 1*s.* net.
The same. In Paper Covers. £ 1.

With the Dutch in the East. See: Cool.

Wright (W.) — The Book of Jonah in four Semitic versions. Chaldee, Syriac, Aethiopic and Arabic. With corresponding glossaries. 8vo. Cloth. pp. 148. 4*s.*

Wynkoop (J. D.) — Manual of Hebrew Syntax. Translated from the Dutch by C. VAN DEN BIESEN. 8vo. Cloth. pp. XXII, 152 and Index. 2*s.* 6*d.* net.

"It is a book, which every Hebrew student should possess, ... we recommend it for general usefulness, and thank Dr. van den Biesen for giving it to the English reader." — *Jewish World.*

"It is one of those books which will become indispensable to the English student who will desire to become acquainted with the construction of Hebrew syntax .... this takes a high rank and will undoubtedly become a general text book on the subject in many colleges and universities."
American Hebrew News.

Wynkoop (J. D.) — Hebrew Grammar. Translated from the Dutch by C. VAN DEN BIESEN. 8vo. Cloth. 2*s.* 6*d.* net.

Yatawara (J. B.) — The Ummaga Yataka, translated into English. *In the Press.*

FOREIGN AND ORIENTAL BOOKS.

Messrs. LUZAC & Co. having Agents in all the principal Towns of the Continent, America and the East, are able to supply any Books not in stock at the shortest notice and at the most reasonable terms.

Subscriptions taken for all Foreign, American and Oriental Periodicals.

LIST OF INDIAN GOVERNMENT PUBLICATIONS.

Messrs. LUZAC & Co. are Official Agents for the sale of the Indian Government Publications.

Acts of the several Governments in India. Different dates and prices.
Aden Gazetteer. By Captain F. M. Hunter. 1877. 5*s*.
Adi Granth. By E. Trumpp. 1877. £ 1.
Agriculture, Report on Indian. By J. A. Voelcker, Ph. D. 1893. 3*s*. 6*d*.
Annals of the Calcutta Botanic Gardens:
I. Monograph on Ficus. Part 1. 1887. £ 1 5*s*.
" " Part 2. 1888. £ 2.
" " Appendix. 1889. 10*s*. 6*d*.
II. Species of Artocarpus, &c. 1889. £ 1 12*s* 6*d*.
III. Species of Pedicularis, &c. 1891. £ 3 10*s*.
IV. Anonaceæ of British India. 1893. £ 3 10*s*.
V., Part 1. A Century of Orchids. Memoir of W. Roxburgh. 1895. £ 3 3*s*. coloured, £ 1 12*s*. 6*d*. uncoloured.
V., Part 2. A Century of New and Rare Indian Plants. 1896. £ 1 12*s*. 6*d*.
VI., Part 1. Turgescence of Motor Organs of Leaves. Parasitic species of Choanephora. 1895. £ 1 10*s*.
VII. Bambuseæ of British India. 1896. £ 2.
Anwar-i-Soheli. By Colonel H. S. Jarrett. 1880. 15*s*.
Archæological Survey of India. (New Series):
IX. South Indian Inscriptions. By E. Hultzsch, Ph.D. Vol. I. 1890. 4*s*.
X. " " " " Vol. II, Part. 1. 1891. 3*s*. 6*d*.

South Indian Inscriptions. By E. Hultzsch, Ph.D. Vol. II, Part 2. 1892. 3*s.* 6*d.*

South Indian Inscriptions. By E. Hultzsch, Ph.D. Vol. II, Part 3. 1895. 5*s.* 6*d.*

XI. Sharqî Architecture of Jaunpur. By A. Führer, Ph.D. 1889. £ 1 1*s.* 6*d.*

XII. Monumental Antiquities in the North-West Provinces. By A. Führer, Ph.D. 1891. 13*s.* 6*d.*

XV. South Indian Buddhist Antiquities. By A. Rea. 1894. 12*s.* 6*d.*

XVII. Architectural, &c. Remains in Coorg. By A. Rea. 1894. 2*s.*

XVIII. The Moghul Architecture of Fatehpur Sikri. By E. W. Smith. Part 1. 1894. £ 1 5*s.*

The Moghul Architecture of Fatehpur Sikri By E. W. Smith. Part 2. 1896. 17*s.* 6*d.*

XXI. Châlukyan Architecture. By A. Rea. 1896. £ 1 2*s.*

XXIII. Muhammadan Architecture in Gujarat. By J. Burgess, C.I.E., LL.D. 1896. £ 1.

Army List, The Indian. Quarterly. 4*s.*

Art Ware, Photographs of Madras and Burmese. 1886. £ 1 15*s.*

Arzis: Bengali, Canarese, Hindi, Mahratta, Malayalam, Tamil, Telugu, and Urdu. 7*s.* 6*d.* each.

Translations of the above (except Hindi). 7*s.* 6*d.* each.

Beer Casks, Destruction of, by a Boring Beetle. By W. F. H. Blandford. 1893. 6*d.*

Bibliographical Index of Indian Philosophical Systems. By F. Hall. 1859. 9*s.*

Bihar Peasant Life. By G. A. Grierson, Ph.D., C.I.E. 1885. 6*s.* 6*d.*

Bihari Language, Seven Grammars of. By G. A. Grierson, Ph.D. C.I.E. (8 parts). 1883—87. £ 1.

Bihari, The Satsaiya of. Edited by G. A. Grierson, Ph.D., C.I.E. 1896. 7*s.* 6*d.*

Bombay Gazetteer, Edited by J. M. Campbell, LL.D., C.I.E.:

I. (Not yet published). — II. Surat and Broach. 1877. 5*s.* 6*d.* — III. Kaira and Panch Mahals. 1879. 2*s.* 6*d.* — IV. Ahmedabad. 1879. 3*s.* — V. Cutch, Palanpur, and Mahi Kantha. 1880. 4*s.* — VI. Rewa Kantha, Narukot, Cambay, and Surat States. 1880. 3*s.* — VII. Baroda. 1883. 5*s.* — VIII. Kathiawar. 1884. 6*s.* 6*d.* — IX. (Not yet published). — X. Ratnagiri and Savantvadi. 1880. 5*s.* — XI. Kolaba and Janjira. 1883. 5*s.* — XII. Khandesh. 1880. 6*s.* — XIII. Thana. (2 parts). 1882. 8*s.* — XIV. Thana: places of interest. 1882. 5*s.* — XV. Kanara. (2 parts). 1883. 7*s.* 6*d.* — XVI. Nasik. 1883. 6*s.* 6*d.* — XVII. Ahmadnagar. 1884. 7*s.* — XVIII. Poona. (3 parts). 1885. 15*s.* 6*d.* — XIX. Satara. 1885. 6*s.* 6*d.* — XX. Sholapur. 1884. 5*s.* — XXI. Belgaum. 1884. 6*s.* — XXII. Dharwar. 1884. 7*s.* 6*d.* — XXIII. Bijapur. 1884. 6*s.* 6*d.* — XXIV. Kolhapur. 1886. 5*s.* — XXV. Botany of the Presidency. 1886. 4*s.* 6*d.* — XXVI. Materials for a Statistical of Bombay Town and Island, Parts I., II., and III. 1893—94. 5*s.* each.

British Burma Gazetteer. Edited by H. R. Spearman. (2 vols.) 1879—80. £ 1 13*s.* 6*d.*

Buddha Gaya; the Hermitage of Sakya Muni. By Rajendralal Mitra. 1878. £ 3.

Burmese, Tables for the Transliteration of, into English. 1896. 1*s.*

Catalogue of the India Office Library, Vol. I (with Index). 1888. 10*s*. 6*d*.
" " " (Supplement). 1895. 5*s*.
" of the Arabic MSS. in the India Office Library. By O. Loth. 1877. 15*s*.
" of the Mandalay MSS. in the India Office Library. By V. Fausböll. 1897. 2*s*.
" of the Pali MSS. in the India Office Library. By H. Oldenberg. 1882. 5*s*.
" of the Sanskrit MSS. in the India Office Library. By Dr. J. Eggeling. (Parts I to V). 1887—96. 10*s*. 6*d*. each.
" of Sanskrit MSS., Bikanir. By Rajendralal Mitra. 1880. 3*s*.
" " " Tanjore. By A. C. Burnell. 1880. £1 11*s*. 6*d*.
" of MSS. in Oudh. By A. Sprenger 1854. 15*s*.

Chestnuts, Papers on Spanish. With Introduction by Sir George Birdwood, K. C. I., C. S. I. 1892. 1*s*.

Cholera, What can the State do to prevent is? By Dr. J. M. Cunningham. 1884. 3*s*.

Coorg Gazetteer. 1884. 5*s*.

Corpus Inscriptionum Indicarum:
I. Inscriptions of Asoka. By Major-General Sir A. Cunningham, K. C. I. E., C. S. I. 1877. 9*s*. 6*d*.
II. (Not yet published.)
III. Inscriptions of the early Gupta King. By J. F. Fleet, C. I. E. 1889. £1 13*s*. 6*d*. with plates. £1 without plates.

Covenanted Civil Servants, Manual of Rules applicable to. Second edition. 1891. 2*s*. 6*d*.

Dictionary of Indian Economic Products. By Dr. Geo Watt, C. I. E. (6 vols. in 9). 1889—93. £3 3*s*.
Ditto, Index to. 1896. 3*s*.

Durga puja. By Pratapa Chandra Ghosha. 1871. 6*s*.

English-Sanskrit Dictionary. By Sir M. Monier-Williams, K. C. I. E. 1851. £1 10*s*.

Fibres. Report on Indian. By C. F. Cross, E. J. Bevan, &c. 1887. 5*s*.

Finance and Revenue Accounts of the Government of India. Annual volumes. 2*s*. 6*d*. each.

Forest Working Plans. By W. E. D'Arcy. (Second edition). 1892. 1*s*. 6*d*.

Fort St. George Diary and Consultation Books: 1681 (Selection) 1893. 3*s*. 6*d*. — 1682. 1894. 4*s*. — 1683. 1894. 5*s*. 6*d*. — 1684. 1895. 5*s*. 6*d*. — 1685. 1895. 7*s*.

Geological Survey Department Publications.

Glossary of Indian Terms. By H. H. Wilson. 1855. £1 10*s*.

Hastings, Warren, Selections from the Records of the Foreign Department relating to the Administration of. Edited by G. W. Forrest, B. A. (3 vols.) 1890. 16*s*.
" " The Administration of. (A reprint of the Introduction to the foregoing.) By G. W. Forrest, B. A. 1892. 5*s*. 6*d*.

India Office Marine Records, List of. 1896. 5*s*.

Kachin Language, Handbook of the. By H. F. Hertz. 1895. 1*s*.

Lansdowne, Lord, The Administration of. By G. W. Forrest, B. A. 1894. 2*s*. 6*d*.
Lepcha Grammar. By Colonel G. P. Mainwaring. 1876. 3*s*.
Lighthouse Construction and Illumination, Report on. By F. W. Ashpitel. 1895. £ 1 9*s*. 6*d*.

Madras District Manuals (revised issues:)
South Canara (2 vols.) 1894. 4*s*.
North Arcot (2 vols.) 1895. 6*s*.
Malabar Manual. By W. Logan. (3 vols.) 1891. £ 1 2*s*. 6*d*.
Manava-Kalpa-Sutra. By Th. Goldstücker. 1861. £ 3.
Manual of Hydraulics. By Captain H. D. Love, R. E. 1890. 5*s*.
Marathi Dictionary. By J. T. Molesworth. 1857. 16*s*.
Marathi Grammar. By the Rev. Ganpatrao R. Navalkar. (Third edition.) 1894. 10*s*. 6*d*.
Meteorological Department Publications.
Muntakhabat-i-Urdu. (Second edition.) 1887. 1*s*. 10*d*.
Mutiny, the Indian, Selections from the Records of the Military Department relating to. Edited by G. W. Forrest, B. A. Vol. I. 1893. 12*s*. 6*d*.

North-East Frontier of Bengal, Relations of the Government with the Hill Tribes of the. By Sir Alexander Mackenzie, K. C. S. I. 1884. 6*s*. 6*d*.
North-West Provinces Gazetteer:
I. Bundelkhand, 1874. 8*s*. 6*d*. — II. Meerut Part. I. 1875. 6*s*. 6*d*. — III. Meerut, Part. II. 1876. 8*s*. 6*d*. — IV. Agra, Part. I. 1876. 8*s*. 6*d*. — V. Rohilkhand. 1879. 8*s*. 6*d*. — VI. Cawnpore, Gorakhpur and Basti. 1881. 9*s*. — VII. Farukhabad and Agra. 1884. 8*s*. — VIII. Muttra, Allahabad and Fatehpur. 1884. 10*s*. — IX. Shahjahanpur, Moradabad aud Rampur Native State. 1883. 8*s*. — X. Himalayan Districts, Part. I. 1882. 13*s*. — XI. Himalayan Districts, Part. II. 1884. 12*s*. 6*d*. — XII. Himalayan Districts Part. III. 1886. 12*s*. — XIII. Azamgarh, Ghazipur and Ballia' 1883. 8*s*. — XIV. Benares, Mirzapur and Jaunpur. 1884. 10*s*.

Oudh Gazetteer. (3 vols.) 1877—78. £ 1.

Paintings, &c. in the India Office, Descriptive Catalogue of. By W. Forster. 1893. 1*s*.
Prakrita Prakasa. By E. B. Cowell. 1854. 9*s*.
Prem Sagar. By E. B. Eastwick. 1851. 15*s*.

Rajputana Gazetteer. (3 vols.) 1879—80. 15*s*.
Rigveda Sanhita. Vols. IV to VI. By Professor Max Müller. 1862—74. £ 2 12*s*. 6*d*. per volume.
Index to ditto. £ 2 5*s*.
Rigveda Translations. By H. H. Wilson. Vols I, III and IV. 1850—66. 13*s*. 6*d*. per volume.
Vols. V and VI. 1888. 18*s*. per volume.

Sanskritt MSS. in S. India, First and Second Reports on. By Dr. Hultzsch. 1895—96. 1*s*. 8*d*. each.
Scientific Memoirs by Medical Officers of the Indian Army:
Part I. 1885. 2*s*. 6*d*. — Part II. 1887. 2*s*. 6*d*. — Part III. 1888.

4*s.* — Part IV. 1889. 2*s.* 6*d.* — Part V. 1890. 4*s.* — Part VI. 1891. 4*s.* — Part VII. 1892. 4*s.* — Part VIII. 1893. 4*s.* — Part IX. 1895. 4*s.*

Selections from the Records of the Burmese Hluttaw. 1889. 6*s.*

Sikkim Gazetteer. By H. H. Risley, C. I. E., and others. 1894. 12*s.* 6*d.*

Specimens of Languages in India. By Sir G. Campbell, K. C. S. I. 1874. £ 1. 16*s.*

Survey Department Publications.

Surveys 1875—90, Memoir on the Indian. By C. E. D. Black. 1891. 7*s.* 6*d.*

Tamil Papers. By Andrew Robertson. 1890. 4*s.*

Technical Art Series of Illustrations of Indian Architectural Decorative Work for the use of Art Schools and Craftsmen:

1886—87. (6 plates.) 2*s.* — 1888—89. (18 plates.) 6*s.* — 1890. (12 plates.) 4*s.* — 1891. (18 plates.) 6*s.* — 1892. (13 plates.) 4*s.* 6*d.* — 1893. (12 plates) 4*s.* — 1894. (14 plates.) 5*s.* — 1895. (12 plates.) 4*s.* — 1896. (15 plates.) 4*s.*

Telegu Reader. By C. P. Brown. (2 vols.) 1852. 14*s.*

Textile Manufactures and Costumes of the People of India. By Dr. Forbes. Watson. 1866. £ 1. 1*s.*

Tibetan-English Dictionary. By H. A. Jaeschke. 1881. £ 1.

Timber, Mensuration of. By P. J. Carter. 1893. 1*s.*

Tobacco. Cultivation and Preparation of, in India. By Dr. Forbes Watson. 1871. 5*s.*

Tombs or Monuments in Bengal, Inscriptions on. Edited by C. R. Wilson, M.A. 1896. 3*s.* 6*d.*

Vikramarka, Tales of. By Ravipati Gurumurti. 1850. 1*s.*

Yield tables of the Scotch Pine. By W. Schlich, Ph. D. 1889. 1*s.*

N.B. In addition to the above, a large number of departmental reports, &c., are on sale at the various Government presses in India. These publications are not kept in stock at the India Office; but should copies of them be required, they will be furnished (on payment), as far as possible, from the supply received for official purposes.

In all cases applications for publications must be made through the official agents.

INDEX OF PRIVATE NAMES.

LUZAC'S ORIENTAL LIST.

NOTICE TO OUR READERS.

With this number we enter upon the eighth year of the publication of our «Oriental List." Four years ago in the first number of our fourth volume we thanked our readers for the generous support we had received from various quarters, including some flattering notices in our contemporaries referring to the value of our «List", and we now tender our thanks to an extended circle of readers. Within recent years the number of works on oriental subjects has increased enormously, and our «List" was started with the object of furnishing a record of such works which should be published at regular intervals. Our aim has therefore been to give each month a complete list of oriental books published in England, on the Continent, in the East and in America, while under the heading «Notes and News" we have endeavoured to give a faithful account of the progress made during the month in the various branches of oriental learning, literature and archaeology. The encouragement we have continuously received from the beginning of the undertaking emboldens us to believe that the «List" has really supplied a want on the part of those who from taste or profession are interested in the languages, literatures and antiquities of the East, and we therefore venture to appeal to our readers who are in the habit of consulting our «List" when making out their orders to send them to us direct.

LONDON, Jan. '98. LUZAC & Co.

PRINTED BY E. J. BRILL, LEYDEN (HOLLAND).